SOFI'S AEGEAN KITCHEN

A Light

Approach to

Traditional

Greek

Home Cooking

SOFI'S AEGEAN KITCHEN

SOFI LAZARIDES KONSTANTINIDES
with HELEN NEWTON HARTUNG

Illustrations by Steven Salerno

CLARKSON POTTER/PUBLISHERS
NEW YORK

To Georgie

Published by Clarkson N. Potter, Inc., 201 East 50th Street, New York, New York 10022. Member of the Crown Publishing Group. Random House, Inc. New York, Toronto, London, Sydney, Auckland

CLARKSON POTTER, POTTER, and colophon are trademarks of Clarkson N. Potter, Inc.

Manufactured in the United States of America

LIBRARY OF CONGRESS CATALOGING-IN-PUBLICATION DATA
Konstantinides, Sofi Lazarides.
  Sofi's Aegean kitchen: a light approach to traditional Greek home cooking / Sofi Lazarides Konstantinides; with Helen Newton Hartung.—1st ed.
    p.   cm.
  Includes index.
  1. Cookery, Greek.   I. Hartung, Helen Newton.   II. Title.
TX723.5.G8K597   1993
641.59495—dc20   92-41104
                                                              CIP

ISBN 0-517-57642-2

10 9 8 7 6 5 4 3 2 1

First Edition

CONTENTS

ACKNOWLEDGMENTS

Sharing food with friends is my passion. Cooking has never been a solitary pursuit for me, and writing this book about cooking certainly wasn't, either. I'd like to express my gratitude and appreciation to all the people who worked with me to make this book come together.

Gerry Furth helped me get started on the long process of putting my ideas about Greek cooking onto paper. Roberta Dean tasted all the results and helped me refine the recipes further.

Helen Newton Hartung, my co-writer, came to feel almost Greek herself as she helped me find just the right words for my thoughts. Carolyn Hart Bryant, my patient editor, believed in the book throughout its long gestation. And speaking of gestation, I'd also like to thank the *four* babies born during this project—one to Helen, one to me, and two to Carolyn—for their understanding of our divided attentions.

My husband, Konstantin, has been a source of unfailing love, inspiration, and support, especially in bringing my dream of a restaurant to life. He must have inherited these family traits from George and Alice Konstantinides, my parents-in-law, whose generous encouragement of all my endeavors—including the creation of the restaurant and this cookbook—has been invaluable.

The staff at Sofi's has contributed much helpful advice. I'd like to thank Nikos Stefanidis, George Spanos, George Hadjiefthimiou, and especially Dimitri Kotsaras for his continuing challenge to strive for the best.

Special thanks go to George Christy, Rose Dosti, Karen Kaplan, Merrill Schindler, Paul Wallach, and the other restaurant writers whose words of praise have helped Sofi's thrive.

I'm also grateful to my friend Dr. Walter Fox, who provided both a wise sounding board and a willing palate.

Last, I would like to thank my parents, Lazaros and Kalliopi Lazarides, for giving me their unconditional love and the inspiration to fulfill my dreams.

FOREWORD

My first memories of Sofi go back to when we were children playing together with our friends in the living room of her large house in Greece. Our games always seemed to end in the kitchen. The cook, a middle-aged village woman with a harsh accent, would beg us to leave her alone. She would bribe us with whatever she happened to be cooking, in whatever its stage of preparation; that was her revenge. Sofi would frequently ask for a more well cooked piece, sometimes making suggestions—such as altering the quantities of certain ingredients—which were never to the cook's liking. It was then that the cook would yell to the nearest adult for help.

Years later, as teen-agers, Sofi's groupies and I would go to her house after school to study, and for *the ritual*. Sofi would often search for what she called "hidden treasure" among the old clothes, linens, and the like packed away in chests in her mother's attic. The "treasure" was scraps of oily paper Sofi found that contained scribbles resembling food recipes. Sofi would announce that they were of a certain age, say forty years old, and that we were all going back forty years in time. Then we would reenact the period while Sofi cooked one of her newfound recipes. (Fortunately she improvised, as some of the "recipes" were notes that belonged to Sofi's uncle, who had been a pharmacist.) Sofi would provide a culinary critique of the dish while we ate. A simple and effective time machine.

We grew up. I came to America to study, and Sofi, now an organic chemist, went on to premed school. We met again after she married Konstantin Konstantinides and moved to Los Angeles, where I was working for my Ph.D. Our life-styles had changed, but we did share a keen interest in good food. Sofi was ecstatic over all the food choices available in this multicultural city. For about a year we would visit religiously, one after the other, the different restaurants listed in a guide she owned. In the meantime, she was preparing to go back to her medical career.

Then, one day, it just happened.

"Costas, I want to open a restaurant."

"You are crazy. Your father will kill you. Your mother will kill you. And if they don't, I will."

"It is what I always wanted to do."

"You always liked to cook. You can cook as a doctor, as a chemist, as a pharmacist. You don't have to become a real cook. What does Konstantin say?"

"He will quit his career as an architect to help. Really."

I hung up. It was too early in the morning. Another one of Sofi's jokes. But Konstantin called me later to say that he was indeed quitting his job to open the restaurant. He assured me that he had thought it through.

The rest is history. Konstantin and Sofi first opened a small restaurant on Robertson Boulevard. The name was, what else, Sofi. For us, Sofi's new groupies—yes, Sofi has a knack for forming circles of devotees—it was the Sofaki, the "small Sofi." The seating capacity was about twenty. Sofi was the cook and also served as a waiter. Konstantin was the maître d'. Every Saturday there was a line of people a block long waiting to get in.

What was it that attracted people to Sofaki? The stunning interior design, the food, Sofi's and Konstantin's gregarious personalities? A combination of all three? Maybe it was Sofi's magical powers derived from strange ingredients that she had discovered in those old scraps of paper. . . .

Next came the present Sofi's, in itself a feast for the senses. While you eat, a life-size bust of a horse—a replica of the figure that can be seen in the Parthenon's frieze—watches over. The piano player plays Greek music. Aromas from the garden penetrate the room. Your waiter (most of them here are of Greek extraction) engages you in a discussion about the art of the latter Byzantine period. Sofi walks by and greets you. And when you taste the food, even if you have never before eaten Greek food, you have no choice but to love it.

In science, we say that discovery is looking at what everybody else has looked at and seeing what nobody else has seen. Innovative cooking is very similar. It is cooking what everybody else has cooked but producing something that tastes unlike any other dish that has come before. And that defines this book's spirit, endowed with a combination of the culture of generations of Greek cooking and Sofi's alchemy.

A dish is worth a thousand words. Enjoy preparing and tasting the wonderful recipes Sofi shares with you. Write your favorite one on a scrap of paper and hide it in your chest of drawers. You never know who will discover it.

—COSTAS SYNOLAKIS, PROFESSOR, SCHOOL OF ENGINEERING, UNIVERSITY OF SOUTHERN CALIFORNIA

INTRODUCTION

When I think back to my childhood in the placid town of Karditsa, in the heart of the Greek mainland, warm memories come flooding back: mornings spent walking amid the wild mountain herbs and flowers; accompanying my father, a doctor, from house to house on his calls; or helping my mother bake traditional crescent-shaped nut cookies at Christmastime.

For me, however, even stronger than the mental pictures these memories summon up are the aromas—of the fragrant wild thyme beneath my feet; of the briny, home-packed olives one of my father's patients would always press on us as we left; of the warm, toasted almonds heaped in big bowls in our whitewashed kitchen.

Even walking to school through town was a sensory experience. Every corner held a bakery, inside of whose warm, foggy windows rested stacks of fragrant, crusty bread. I knew my mother would save the golden end of one of these loaves for me when I came home from school, so I could sprinkle our fruity olive oil over it and eat it with a chunk of feta cheese.

Food—choosing it, cooking it, and most of all savoring it—seems inextricably wound up in my life. During my childhood, appreciating good food was even more central to Greek life than usual, since the country had just recovered from the civil war that devastated Greece right after World War II. Being able to enjoy Christmas and Easter with a dining table full of delicious things to eat was a blessing we never took for granted.

In addition, food was not only our nourishment; it was the main form of entertainment in our small town. There was no television and movie theaters were rare, so social events consisted of inviting people over to eat, and spending long hours around tables filled with the best the house had to offer.

My mother, a housewife like all Greek women of her day, was well known for her culinary talent and great hospitality. I learned much from her, just as she learned from her mother; the techniques are handed down from generation to generation.

Actually, I am very lucky because there were notable cooks on both sides of my large family, among them my mother's aunts Vita and Georgia (my grandmother's sisters), who lived in Volos, a beautiful city on the Pagassaean Gulf of the Aegean Sea. It was only about three hours away from our town of Karditsa, so we visited them almost every weekend.

Only the best was good enough for Vita and Georgia. Vita, in charge of the shopping, would insist on buying fish that had been caught that day and meat the butcher cut in front of her own eyes. She would make *mousaka* only during the brief time when eggplant was at its ripest, and she always tasted any fruit at the market before she would buy it.

Georgia oversaw the presentation of the dishes. She would never bring food to the table unless she decorated the platter first, even for the most casual meals. Both Vita's and Georgia's insistence on high quality made a lasting impression on me.

And then there was my uncle Lakis, my mother's brother, who lived in Thessaloniki, a northern city in Macedonia. He was a charming bachelor who loved living well and eating well. He used to take my sister and me to fine restaurants and urge us to try things we'd never eaten before, such as roasted head of pork or stuffed mussels. With his encouragement, I began to develop my own taste.

On my father's side there was my aunt Harikleia. I ate at her house often, and it was always an unforgettable experience because Harikleia was such a gifted cook, especially when it came to fyllo pies. I used to spend hours watching her. "Don't just look at me," she would say as she worked rapidly on the tender sheets of fyllo dough. "Food is to touch. Feel it, put it in your mouth, taste it! Don't be afraid to play with it—it doesn't bite!"

I inherited my love of food from my family, to be sure, but the more I learned about my native cuisine, the more I realized that it is almost impossible to be Greek and not have an inbred feeling for food—if not for creating it, at least for appreciating it! Even the earliest records of our culture document an interest in food. There are references to recipes in writings that date back as far as the 8th century B.C. By the time of Alexander the Great (356–323 B.C.) there were already cooking schools and professional chefs; Greek cooking had become a true art.

Always in Greek life, food and religion have been intertwined. Ancient Greeks erected temples to Aedifia, the goddess of good eating, and offered special devotions to Dionysus, the god of wine. Nowadays, the tradition of the Orthodox Christian Church dictates special menus for holidays such as Christmas, Easter, and Lent.

My own belief is that there is no other country, past or present, where people are as connected to food from the moment they are born to the day they die. I can hardly recall a single important event in my life that didn't include food. For example, the day my younger sister Elena was born, my aunt Harikleia ran all around the neighborhood, bringing people the *synharikia* (good news), along with all kinds of homemade treats such as candied fruits and spoon desserts. She even prepared one of her best fyllo pies for my mother and the rest of the family.

Then there was the day that Harikleia's husband, Stefanos, died. Women crowded into her kitchen to help her cook the big meal that would follow the funeral. I can't explain how someone so overcome with grief could muster all the energy required to prepare this meal. But Greeks like to say good-bye the same way they welcome their loved ones into the world—with plenty of food. According to tradition, the bereaved must offer relatives and friends the most carefully prepared meal possible, always including *Spanokopita* (Spinach Pie, page 132) and lots of dry red wine, laid out on one or three tables, never two or four, so that they will forgive the faults and remember the virtues of the departed loved one.

Happier times have their own protocol as well, and I have countless warm memories of the food that was the focus of our family Christmas dinners, Easter parties, and weddings. For example, a week before a traditional Greek wedding, the bride's family serves *glyka* (sweets) to everyone who stops by to see the dowry of handwoven linens, blankets, and so on. After the marriage ceremony, the groom takes the bride to his parents' home, where his mother feeds them a spoonful of a dessert, usually white for the occasion, so their life will be sweet and smooth. At the party that follows wine is plentiful, and platters brim with regional specialties. On the mainland, dishes such as roasted lamb and goat with rice and fyllo pies, including *Tyropitakia* (Cheese Triangles, page 22), *Kreatopita* (Meat Pie, page 139), and *Galatopita* (Milk Pie, page 143), are most common. For weddings on Crete and some of the other Aegean islands, the most gifted cooks prepare the delicate *Xerotigana* —fritters shaped like open flowers, dipped in honey syrup and piled in baskets. This "dessert of joy," as it is called, is served only on happy occasions.

I think it was this profound connection to food that I experienced growing up in Greece that gave me the impetus to open my restaurant in America. After my marriage to Konstantin in 1982, we moved to a quiet suburb of Los Angeles. I didn't speak English very well and I didn't know very many people, so I assuaged my loneliness by cooking the comforting, familiar foods of my homeland. Of course, being Greek, I cooked huge quantities and invited neighbors to try the results. My new friends, liking what they tasted, began asking me to cook for parties. Then one day Konstantin and I walked past a charming Indian restaurant with a terrace and five tables. I knew instantly that it would make a perfect Greek cafe. The owner was willing to sell and, with the help of Konstantin and his parents, I embarked on my career as a restaurateur.

The first few months were chaotic: the tiny kitchen was upstairs and I was constantly running between it and my five tables downstairs. I knew nothing about American tastes. "How do you expect to run a restaurant if you've never heard of iced tea?" one early customer demanded. A glowing review in a local paper nearly did me in—lines formed around the block and I couldn't cook fast enough. But I added iced tea to the menu, moved to larger quarters (with a larger, tree-shaded terrace), hired some help, and have been happily introducing more and more people to my lighter, fresher Greek food ever since.

As I began thinking about this book, I realized that the one common thread in Greek cooking from all regions is spontaneity. No two Greek women ever cook the same, not even mother and daughter. A dish is always influenced by the cook's individual tastes, experience, and mood. (So don't ever try to check a Greek recipe with more than one of your Greek friends!)

Another thing I have learned is that the Greek way of eating is an inherently healthy one. In fact, one message I hope to communicate in this book is that Greek food, properly prepared, is not the heavy cuisine some people seem to think it is. For example, Greeks traditionally eat red meat only once or twice a week. The Greek Orthodox Church decrees that Wednesdays and Fridays are vegetarian days, and chicken and fish are usually served on the other days. Also, Greeks end most meals simply, with fruit; elaborate sweets are saved for special occasions.

Olive oil, which is perhaps the most important ingredient in Greek cooking, is unsaturated and considered healthier than most other kinds of fat. Nevertheless, modern tastes prefer less fat and lower calorie counts than you'd find in traditional Greek dishes. Consequently, I've substantially reduced the amount of olive oil in my versions of the recipes. I've shortened cooking times for many seafood and vegetable recipes, and I've also reduced the amount of butter that goes between the leaves of fyllo dough in pies. The syrup that covers many Greek desserts can be sticky and heavy; mine has much less sugar.

But most important for health, I've learned to follow the ancient Greek maxim, "Everything in moderation." This allows me to enjoy the delicious Greek *mezethes* (array of appetizers)—only I serve three kinds rather than ten. I can still eat rich and crusty fyllo pies—just not every day. And I save the big desserts—the *Baklava* (page 154) and the *Galactoboureko* (Custard Fyllo Pie, page 158)—for special events.

You don't have to be Greek, or a professional cook, to prepare my dishes. You do have to be enthusiastic though, and smile as you cook. Use your simplest cooking utensils and the very best-quality ingredients. I guarantee success. And never forget my aunt Harikleia's advice: "Don't be afraid to play with food. It doesn't bite!"

SOFI'S AEGEAN KITCHEN

STOCKING THE GREEK KITCHEN

When I was growing up in Greece, women shopped each morning for most of the day's food. String bags in hand, they would head for the produce stands to pick what was freshest and in season. Then came a visit to the butcher or fishmonger—that is, if it wasn't a meatless day or if they weren't planning to catch and pluck chickens from their own backyard.

On meatless days—Wednesdays and Fridays and many holidays, as decreed by the Greek Orthodox Church—housewives would often turn to their large supplies of dried beans to make a nourishing and filling family dinner. They could also draw on their year's supply of olive oil, which they bought from the local olive oil producer and stored in large crocks in their homes. Their kitchens were hung with dried herbs from their own gardens, and their larders were full of preserves they had put up in season.

Nowadays, while few people have the time or the energy to shop and cook as was done in the past, I feel that we can still learn something from the old ways. My mother and aunts taught me to approach marketing with a certain amount of flexibility; if the shrimp they were seeking, for example, didn't seem to be of the highest quality, they changed their menu plans. I do the same.

Another thing I learned from my mother is the importance of maintaining a well-stocked pantry. She was always able to serve delicious tidbits to guests or a nourishing family dinner simply by putting together ingredients from her larder. What follows is a list of the basics to be found in any Greek kitchen.

OLIVE OIL: This is the most important pantry item of all. While none of us would want to buy a year's supply at once, as my mother did, I do keep plenty on hand, both extra-virgin and pure olive oil. I use the flavorful, extra-virgin olive oil, with its fruity taste and green, slightly murky appearance, in salads or in lightly cooked dishes. It is very difficult to find Greek extra-virgin olive oil in the United States, as it is produced locally in very small quantities. You can use Italian extra-virgin instead. The less-expensive pure olive oil is what we use for cooking over higher heats or for dishes requiring longer cooking times. Pure Greek olive oil is usually not hard to find in large supermarkets, gourmet stores, or Middle Eastern markets. I also keep a supply of corn oil or safflower oil for frying.

OLIVES: These are another essential ingredient to have on hand. They are almost always part of the *mezethes*, or appetizer course, and are used in many recipes. The most well-known Greek olives come from the area of Kalamata in the southern Peloponnesus. Calamata olives are oblong with pointed ends, and they are often stored in their own oil rather than in brine. Other types of Greek olives are round and packed in brine, or dried and salted. Usually I don't recommend buying canned olives; it is far better to buy olives from a reputable deli or food shop that stocks them in large jars of brine. The exception is Calamata olives; because they are produced in such quantity and are often packed in their own oil, they usually hold up well in cans.

VINEGAR: Greeks use red wine vinegar. Occasionally, for salads I use red wine vinegar infused with thyme, for example, but usually plain red wine vinegar serves every purpose.

DRIED FOODS: A typical Greek pantry will contain a large stock of dried foods. Lentils, garbanzo beans, and lima beans are always on hand. You will usually find several types of pasta—spaghetti, macaroni, and orzo at least —as well as rice. Nuts are considered a basic ingredient in Greek cooking, so I always stock walnuts, almonds, and pine nuts. Raisins and other dried fruits are useful, too.

HERBS AND FLAVORINGS: My mother used to grow her own herbs or pick those growing in the mountains and hang them in her kitchen to dry. I like to use fresh herbs whenever possible, but I also keep a supply of dried ones on hand—essentials are sage, oregano, bay leaves, dill, thyme, rosemary, tarragon, and mint. In my mother's day, no Greek home was complete without a pot of fresh basil growing on the balcony or in the backyard; luckily, fresh basil is now available in supermarkets. Cinnamon, nutmeg, and salt and pepper are basics I always have in my kitchen, and capers round out the spice cabinet. For desserts, we always use vanilla powder rather than vanilla extract; I think the flavor is purer and stronger. Many supermarkets carry vanilla powder, but if you can't find it, I've included amounts for vanilla extract in all the recipes. Sugar and honey are also essentials.

TEA AND COFFEE: I keep a variety of herbal teas in my pantry. We Greeks have favorite herbal infusions for various purposes: *faskomelo* is good for sore throats; and chamomile, which grows wild in the mountains, we give to colicky babies, among other uses. Greeks rarely drink European-style or Chinese tea, preferring coffee. I buy coffee vacuum-packed and pre-ground to keep on hand, because our strong Greek coffee requires an extremely fine grind that is virtually impossible to achieve with a home machine.

PRESERVES: A Greek pantry will always be stocked with our traditional preserves. Made from fruits or certain vegetables in season, these preserves customarily are served to guests along with strong coffee and ice water. Some of them also make wonderful toppings for yogurt or ice cream. We also always stock tomatoes in various forms. My mother used to can her own tomatoes when they were in season. She'd also make sun-dried tomatoes and tomato paste, which she poured into small crocks and covered with olive oil. I simply keep on my shelves good-quality canned tomatoes, tomato paste, and sun-dried tomatoes that I reconstitute in olive oil. I also always have grape leaves, bottled in brine, at hand. These are imported and can usually be found in gourmet sections of supermarkets or in specialty shops. They must be well rinsed before using or else they'll be too salty.

LEMONS: Lemons are such an important part of Greek cooking, I always keep about half a dozen on hand.

DAIRY PRODUCTS: My mother used to shop at a *galaktopoleia* for all her dairy products, but, with the exception of certain cheeses, a supermarket stocks everything you need for Greek cooking. I always keep milk and butter on hand, as well as plain, whole-milk yogurt (use low-fat yogurt if you must, but the flavor will not be the same). Today's ultrapasteurized whipping cream is not as good as the fresh heavy cream I grew up with, but it will do. A good cheese store will provide high-quality *feta* (the packaged grocery-store variety is not as good); *kefalotiri,* or hard grating cheese (you can substitute Parmesan or Romano if kefalotiri is not available), and the milder and creamier-textured *kasseri.* I like to keep a supply of cheeses on hand for nibbling or serving to guests; two favorites in Greece are *graviera* (similar to Gruyère) and *rokfor* (our version of Roquefort).

FYLLO: Commercially made fyllo dough and puff pastry dough are essentials in my freezer. That way I can easily prepare fyllo pies or pastry desserts whenever I wish.

BREAD: I like to serve good, crusty bread with meals. Like vegetables, bread is best when bought fresh each day. Greeks like a variety of breads: *horiatiko populas,* or crusty peasant bread; *mavro,* or brown bread; *lagana,* or white bread; and *starenio,* or whole wheat bread. Greek bakeries are also the source of cookies and sweet biscuits (if we don't make our own) to keep on hand in airtight tins to serve to visitors.

WINE: Most people think of retsina when they think of Greek wine. This white wine is definitely an acquired taste, its sharp resiny flavor coming from the oak barrels in which the wine is aged. Though I always keep retsina on hand, I prefer to drink chardonnay with fish or poultry and a good strong red wine, like a merlot, with lamb or beef. Ouzo, the other famous Greek drink, is a fortified spirit, like vodka or gin, made from grape skins and flavored with anise. It is served over ice as an apéritif and usually accompanied by feta, tomatoes, olives, and sardines. Metaxa is a well-known Greek brandy, similar to French cognac.

Once your pantry shelves are well stocked with these basics, you're ready to try your hand at Greek cooking. You'll already have mastered one essential part of the Greek way of life: you'll always have something delicious to offer a guest, even if it's only olives and cheese!

Appetizers

(Mezethes)

In Greece, an unexpected guest is never really unexpected. The next-door neighbor might drop by; or it might be a distant cousin just passing through; or the friends of friends. Each of these visitors is happily received; according to Greek mythology, Zeus, the king of the gods, commanded his people to welcome any guest, and to this day Greeks consider hospitality an essential virtue.

A visitor who drops by in the morning would certainly expect Greek coffee, accompanied by a serving of preserved fruit, a traditional sweet that every good hostess keeps in her pantry. For anyone visiting in the afternoon or evening, custom dictates a glass of ouzo, our national apéritif. What separates the merely good hostess from the truly inspired one is what she serves with the ouzo.

My mother was such a truly inspired hostess. Though she'd protest that she had nothing special to offer a visitor, "nothing special" to her meant a table filled with fifteen different little dishes prepared within

7

minutes. I never knew how she did it! Sliced cucumber and tomatoes, cubes of kasseri and feta cheeses, Calamata olives and toursia (pickled vegetables), potato salad topped with sliced red onion and hard-boiled eggs, anchovies and sardines, Tzatziki (Yogurt-Cucumber Salad), and slices of crusty bread were just a few of the offerings.

My mother's guests would indulge in what is still probably the favorite Greek way of eating—nibbling. The sorts of things my mother served —an assortment of dips, salads, and bits of chicken, meat, fish, or livers—are called mezethes and are never considered a first course in Greece. Instead, they are served together in the middle of the table.

Mezethes are the key to everyday eating, not only at home but in the kaffenion, the neighborhood cafe, where men spend their free time playing backgammon or cards, and the ouzeria. Usually open at noon and in late evening, ouzerias were for many years hangouts for men, but they are now popular meeting places for sophisticated young Greeks of both sexes. The ouzeria's reputation depends solely on the variety of appetizers it offers. Once the word is out that a particular ouzeria serves truly special mezethes, you can easily wait an hour for a table.

Perhaps everyone's favorite places for mezethes, however, are the open-air, beachfront tavernas that line all the popular seaside resorts. Though their big concrete decks are deserted in the winter, the first warm spring day brings out the wooden chairs and tables, the colorful umbrellas, the crowds—and the mouth-watering smells.

I looked forward every year to the opening of the tavernas. It meant that summer was just around the corner, and I would be spending many weeks at the beautiful beachfront house my uncle Lakis had built at Perea, a resort just half an hour from Thessaloniki.

During the day the beach was filled with people seeking relief from the city heat. Like magic, though, when the sun went down the same crowds somehow all squeezed together at the little tables and chairs of the tavernas. One very popular taverna was called Faliro. The owner's two daughters were good friends of mine and that assured me of at least a couple of treats every time I visited on my bicycle.

Nothing but mezethes were available at Faliro's and other typical beach tavernas, and there were never menus. You ordered by the wonderful smells: fried calamari; steamed langostino; fried baby smelt or octopus. There were all kinds of dips—made of cucumbers and yogurt, or eggplant, or fish roe—that are eaten like salads in Greece, as well as Horiatiki (Greek Village Salad, page 13), roasted red peppers, and a classic salad of boiled greens called Horta Vrasta (page 11).

Now when I go back home I look forward to indulging in this traditional way of eating as soon as I arrive. I can do this just for a while, though, because the endless rounds of sipping ouzo and devouring mezethes can be too much for me. Today I prefer to serve just one or two of these tidbits as an accent to a balanced meal. A couple of them are the perfect complement to apéritifs or make a wonderful first course.

FASOLIA PIAZI *(Baby Lima Bean Salad)*

*For casual meals on warm summer days, Americans have their potato salad.
Greeks have* Fasolia Piazi, *made with baby lima beans.*

1 pound small, dried lima beans
¾ cup extra-virgin olive oil
⅓ cup red wine vinegar
1 medium red onion, finely
   chopped
5 green onions, tops included,
   finely chopped

2 tablespoons finely chopped fresh
   Italian parsley
2 tablespoons finely chopped fresh
   dill
Salt to taste

Put the beans in a large, heavy saucepan. Fill it halfway with water and
bring to a boil over medium heat. Cook, partly covered, over low heat for
about 1 hour, or until beans are tender.

Drain the beans and put them into a serving bowl. Pour the oil and vinegar
over them. Add the red and green onions, parsley, dill, and salt and toss
gently. Cover and refrigerate for at least 1 hour before serving.

SERVES 6

KOKKINES PIPERIES SALATA
(Red Pepper Salad)

Macedonians are known throughout Greece as meraklithes, *or experts on good food
and wine. Their farmlands are rich, and their coastal waters teem with fish, so they
have an abundance of fresh ingredients to draw upon. Red peppers are especially
plentiful, which is why the Greeks call this dish Macedonian Salad. Though
simple, it is delicious.*

6 large sweet red peppers
   Extra-virgin olive oil to taste

Red wine vinegar to taste
Salt to taste

Preheat the oven to 450° F.

Wash and dry the peppers. Put them on a baking sheet and bake until they are soft and their skins start to blacken, about 10 to 15 minutes. Let cool; when they are cool enough to handle, peel away the blackened skins, trim off the stems, and remove the seeds. Arrange the peppers on a plate and sprinkle them with oil and vinegar. Season with salt and serve. The peppers will keep in the refrigerator, covered, for a couple of days.

SERVES 6

HORTA VRASTA *(Cooked Greens Salad)*

In the lush area of Karditsa, where I grew up, wild greens abounded. We could simply go out into the open fields and, armed with small, sharp knives, collect masses of dandelion and rathikia, *a very common wild green. My mother always used to urge these greens on us, insisting on their abundance of vitamins and minerals. Now, however, I don't need any urging to appreciate their tangy flavor. A variety of greens, steamed or boiled and tossed with good-quality oil, makes a great salad.*

2 pounds dandelion greens, curly endive, escarole, or turnip greens	½ teaspoon salt
	7 tablespoons extra-virgin olive oil
	Lemon juice to taste

Wash greens thoroughly. Fill a large pot halfway with water and add salt. Bring to a boil, add greens, and cook, uncovered, over medium heat for about 15 minutes, or until tender but not mushy. Drain and let cool. Place in a serving bowl and toss gently with the olive oil and lemon juice.

SERVES 6

SALATA GIGANDES *(Butter Bean Salad)*

The pale green of butter beans (large lima beans) provides the perfect backdrop for the colorful red onion, tomato, and green pepper tossed together in this salad. As with all salads and cold dishes, extra-virgin olive oil is a key to good flavor.

2 cups cooked butter beans

2 medium ripe tomatoes, peeled, seeded, and diced

1 medium cucumber, peeled and coarsely chopped

1 small sweet green pepper, finely chopped

1 small red onion, peeled and coarsely chopped

4 ounces feta cheese, cut into small cubes (about 1 cup)

2 tablespoons extra-virgin olive oil

1 tablespoon fresh lemon juice
Salt and freshly ground black pepper to taste

Finely chopped fresh Italian parsley for garnish

In a large bowl, combine the beans, tomatoes, cucumber, green pepper, onion, and cheese. In a small bowl, whisk together the oil, lemon juice, and salt and pepper. Pour this over the bean mixture and toss gently. Serve cool, garnished with chopped parsley. This salad will keep, covered, in the refrigerator for up to 3 days.

SERVES 6

LAHANO SALATA *(Cabbage Salad)*

This is simply a Greek version of coleslaw, but instead of mayonnaise, it calls for extra-virgin olive oil and lemon juice. The result is a lighter and tangier salad.

1 medium green cabbage, finely shredded

2 medium carrots, peeled and finely shredded

6 tablespoons extra-virgin olive oil

2 tablespoons lemon juice
Salt to taste

Green and black olives for garnish

In a large salad bowl, mix the cabbage and carrots. Pour the oil and lemon juice over the vegetables and season with salt. Mix well. Serve cool, garnished with olives.

SERVES 6

HORIATIKI *(Greek Village Salad)*

No Greek table is complete without this refreshing summer salad. It also makes a perfect lunch by itself.

3 large, ripe, firm tomatoes, cut in
    wedges
2 medium cucumbers, peeled and
    sliced
1 medium red onion, thinly sliced
1 medium sweet green pepper,
    seeded, ribbed, and thinly
    sliced

½ cup extra-virgin olive oil
5 tablespoons red wine vinegar
  Salt to taste
4 ounces feta cheese, cut into
    small cubes (about 1 cup)

  Calamata olives and dried
    oregano for garnish

In a large bowl, combine tomatoes, cucumbers, onion, and green pepper. In a small bowl, whisk together the oil, vinegar, and salt. Pour this over the vegetables and mix gently. Arrange the feta cheese on top and garnish with olives. Sprinkle with oregano leaves and serve cool.

SERVES 6

PATZARIA ME YIAOURTI *(Beets with Yogurt)*

This lovely winter salad, with its creamy pink dressing bathing cubes of bright red beets, adds a welcome splash of color to the season's table. The walnuts in the recipe reveal its Turkish origins.

1 pound fresh beets, tops removed
3 tablespoons red wine vinegar
½ cup plain yogurt
4 tablespoons extra-virgin olive oil

1 garlic clove, pressed
⅓ cup finely chopped walnuts
Salt to taste

Put the beets in a medium pot and cover with water. Bring to a boil and cook, partly covered, until tender, about 40 minutes. Drain and cool. Peel the beets and cut into medium dice or julienne strips. Transfer the beets to a salad bowl and pour the vinegar over them.

In a small bowl, combine the yogurt, oil, and garlic and stir into the beets. Fold in the walnuts and season with salt. Serve cool.

SERVES 6

ROSSIKI SALATA *(Russian Salad)*

This composed salad has long been a classic in Greek cooking, even though it is called Russian Salad. It looks prettiest when the potatoes and carrots are neatly diced to uniform size.

2 large red or white potatoes,
   boiled or steamed until soft,
   and peeled
2 large carrots, scraped and boiled
   or steamed until tender
1 dill pickle, finely chopped
½ cup cooked green peas

2 tablespoons capers
1 cup mayonnaise

Romaine lettuce leaves and 2
   sliced hard-boiled eggs for
   garnish

Dice the potatoes and carrots and mix with the pickle, peas, and capers. Add the mayonnaise and mix gently but thoroughly.

Arrange the lettuce leaves on a platter and mound the salad on top. Decorate with the sliced eggs. Serve cool. The salad will keep, covered, in the refrigerator for about 3 days.

SERVES 6

ANIXIATIKI *(Spring Salad)*

Usually served around Easter, when new potatoes, baby lettuce, fresh dill, and scallions make their first appearance in the markets, this salad has always signaled the end of winter for me.

1 medium head romaine lettuce, washed and coarsely chopped
4 green onions, including some tops, finely chopped
1 small bunch fresh dill, finely chopped

2 medium potatoes, steamed or boiled until soft, and peeled and diced
½ cup extra-virgin olive oil
4 tablespoons red wine vinegar
2 tablespoons mayonnaise

GARNISH
2 hard-boiled eggs, thinly sliced
1 sour pickle, finely sliced

1 tablespoon capers
Anchovies in oil (optional)

In a large salad bowl, combine the lettuce, green onions, dill, and potatoes. In a small bowl, mix the oil, vinegar, and mayonnaise until smooth. Pour the dressing over the salad and mix gently. Garnish with the eggs, pickle, capers, and anchovies, if desired. Serve cool.

SERVES 6

SALATES *(Marinated Vegetable Salads)*

A dish of fresh, seasonal vegetables marinated in a tangy dressing is popular on the appetizer table in Greece. We always had the following beet and cauliflower salads in winter and green bean and zucchini salads in summer, when those vegetables appeared in our local open-air markets. But here, many of these vegetables are available year-round. I like to make three or four of these simple salads and arrange them on a large platter, like a vegetable antipasto, accompanied by Calamata olives, chunks of feta cheese, and a loaf of crusty bread.

Always use best-quality extra-virgin olive oil for these salads.

PATZAROSALATA *(Beet Salad)*

1 bunch fresh beets, including tops	¼ cup red wine vinegar
⅓ cup extra-virgin olive oil	Salt to taste

Wash the beets including the greens. Trim the greens from the beets and set aside. Put the beets into a large pot, cover with water, and bring to a boil. Cook, covered, over medium heat for about 35 minutes. Add the greens and continue cooking until the beets are tender and the greens have wilted, about 10 minutes. Drain and cool.

Peel the beets and cut them into thick slices. Chop the beet greens into 1-inch pieces. Put the greens and the beets into a large salad bowl, pour the oil and vinegar over them, season with salt, and toss gently. Serve cool.

SERVES 6

KOUNOUPITHI *(Cauliflower Salad)*

1 large cauliflower	Juice of 1 lemon
½ cup extra-virgin olive oil	Salt to taste

Wash the cauliflower and trim off the tough stems. Break the cauliflower into small florets and steam until tender, about 10 to 15 minutes. Place in a serving dish, pour the olive oil and lemon juice over, season with salt, and toss gently. Serve cool.

SERVES 6

ABELOFASOULA SALATA *(Green Bean Salad)*

1½ pounds slender fresh green beans, ends trimmed	⅓ cup red wine vinegar
½ cup extra-virgin olive oil	Salt to taste

Steam the beans until tender, about 5 minutes. Whisk the oil, vinegar, and salt together and pour over the beans. Toss gently. Serve cool.

SERVES 6

KOLOKYTHIA SALATA *(Zucchini Salad)*

12 small, very fresh zucchini	Finely chopped fresh Italian
½ cup extra-virgin olive oil	parsley for garnish
Juice of 1 lemon	
Salt to taste	

Steam the zucchini until tender, about 15 minutes. Place them on a serving platter. Whisk the oil and lemon juice together and pour over the zucchini. Season with salt and garnish with parsley. Serve cool.

SERVES 6

DOLMATHES YALANTZI

(Vegetarian Stuffed Grape Leaves)

My aunt Thalia, a native of Constantinople, was one of the many immigrants who came from Asia Minor to Thessaloniki in the 1920s. These immigrants soon became known for their sophisticated and delicious cooking; they spent many hours reminiscing about the fabulous foods—tomatoes as sweet as peaches, cabbages as big as pumpkins—they left behind in Asia Minor. This recipe was one of Aunt Thalia's favorites. She adapted it from an original recipe in the classic book Loxandra, *about a woman from Constantinople who personified the ideal Greek wife, mother, and hostess.*

Grape leaves preserved in brine are sold from barrels or in jars in Greek or Middle Eastern groceries. The leaves are very salty, so you must rinse them well before using.

1-pound jar of grape leaves preserved in brine	3 tablespoons finely chopped fresh dill
¾ cup pure olive oil	Salt and freshly ground black pepper to taste
3 medium onions, finely chopped	1½ cups warm water
3 cups long-grain white rice	5 tablespoons fresh lemon juice
2 tablespoons finely chopped fresh Italian parsley	

Using plenty of hot water, thoroughly rinse the brine from the preserved grape leaves. Drain them and set aside.

In a large, heavy skillet, heat the oil and sauté the onions until translucent. Add the rice, parsley, dill, salt and pepper, and warm water. Cook, half covered, over low heat for about 10 minutes, stirring occasionally, until rice is half cooked and no liquid remains in the skillet.

To fill, lay the leaves flat on a work surface, shiny side down, and remove the tough stems. Spoon some of the rice mixture onto the widest part of each leaf. Fold up the bottom of leaf, then the sides, and roll it up toward the tip.

Spread a few of the larger, unstuffed leaves on the bottom of a saucepan. Tightly pack the stuffed grape leaves on top of that, folded side down, to keep them from unwrapping. Press a heatproof plate down on top of them so that they don't move while cooking. Cover with hot water and add the lemon juice. Simmer, covered, for about 1 hour, or until the grape leaves are tender and the rice well cooked. Serve warm or cold. Good accompaniments are plain yogurt or *Tzatziki* (Yogurt-Cucumber Salad, page 25).

SERVES 6

KEFTEDES *(Meatballs)*

These meatballs come from my favorite taverna in Volos. In every part of Greece, you'll find a version of meatballs, each seasoned a little differently. What makes these special is the addition of fresh mint. You can use all beef or a combination of ground meats if you like, and accompany the meatballs with roasted potatoes and a Greek salad. Traditionally these are fried, but I think they taste just as good baked.

1 pound ground beef
1 large onion, finely chopped
2 tablespoons finely chopped
    fresh Italian parsley
2 tablespoons finely chopped
    fresh mint
1 teaspoon dried oregano

1 large egg
2 tablespoons pure olive oil
4 slices firm white bread, at least
    2 days old
1 cup all-purpose flour
    Salt and freshly ground black
    pepper to taste

Preheat the oven to 450° F.

In a large bowl, thoroughly combine the beef, onion, parsley, mint, oregano, egg, and olive oil. Dip the bread in water, squeeze to remove excess moisture, and crumble it into the bowl. Mix well. Pinch off pieces of the meat mixture and shape into balls the size of a large walnut. Roll them in the flour.

Place the meatballs on a greased baking sheet and bake for 15 to 20 minutes, turning occasionally, until crisp. Sprinkle with salt and pepper, and serve warm.

MAKES ABOUT 18 MEATBALLS

DOLMATHES AVGOLEMONO
(Meat-Stuffed Grape Leaves with Egg-Lemon Sauce)

These are more substantial than the grape leaves in the preceding recipe. While they are excellent as an appetizer or as part of a buffet, they also make a lovely light luncheon dish, accompanied by a green salad and crusty bread.

¾ pound ground lamb
¾ pound ground beef
1 large onion, finely chopped
1 cup long-grain white rice
⅓ cup pure olive oil
3 tablespoons finely chopped fresh
    Italian parsley

3 tablespoons finely chopped fresh
    dill
Salt and freshly ground black
    pepper to taste
1-pound jar of grape leaves
    preserved in brine

EGG-LEMON SAUCE
¾ cup milk
3 tablespoons cornstarch

3 large eggs
4 tablespoons fresh lemon juice

In a large bowl, mix the meats, onion, rice, oil, parsley, dill, and salt and pepper. Set aside.

Rinse the grape leaves well with plenty of hot water and let them drain. Place shiny side down on a work surface and trim away the tough stems. Spoon about 1 tablespoon of the meat mixture onto the center of each leaf. Turn in the bottom of the leaf and then the sides and roll it up toward the tip.

Cover the bottom of a heavy saucepan with a few of the larger grape leaves or twigs. Stack the stuffed leaves on top, folded side down, crowding them so that they don't move during cooking. Place a heavy heatproof plate on top. Add hot water to cover and simmer over low heat, covered, for about 1 hour, until leaves are tender and rice and meat are cooked. Measure out 2 cups of liquid from the pot and set the grape leaves aside.

To make the sauce, heat the 2 cups of reserved liquid in a small saucepan. In a cup, blend the milk with the cornstarch until smooth. Add it to the hot broth in the saucepan, stirring constantly until the sauce thickens. Turn off the heat.

Beat the eggs and lemon juice in a small bowl until foamy and add gradually to the hot sauce, stirring constantly. The sauce should be yellow and creamy.

Arrange the stuffed grape leaves on a platter and pour the hot sauce over them. Serve immediately. If you wish to reheat the sauce, do so over very low heat, or it will curdle.

SERVES 6

SPETZOFAI *(Sausage and Pepper Sauté)*

In my region of Thessalia, every family raised a pig. The second day after Christmas was the traditional time to butcher the well-fed pig and begin the arduous process of curing the meat and making enough sausage to last all winter. For months after Christmas, patients visiting my father's office would bring along some of their best sausages for the doctor and his family. Depending on the individual cook's recipe, the sausages would be flavored with specks of leeks, red peppers, orange peel, scallions, oregano, thyme, or tarragon. Spetzofai is a specialty unique to Pelion, the mountain region above Volos, and uses a local sausage flavored with spicy, red pepper. You can substitute spicy Italian sausage.

1 tablespoon pure olive oil
1½ pounds spicy sausage links, cut into 1-inch pieces
5 large sweet red peppers, seeded, ribbed, and cut into strips
3 medium ripe tomatoes, peeled, seeded, and diced
1 bunch fresh Italian parsley, finely chopped

In a large skillet, heat the oil and add the sausage and peppers. Sauté for about 5 minutes over high heat, until the peppers are soft and the sausage turns light brown. Discard excess fat. Add the tomatoes and parsley, stir gently, and simmer over low heat, covered, for about 15 to 20 minutes, or until the sauce remaining in the skillet is thick. Serve warm.

SERVES 6

TYROPITAKIA *(Cheese Triangles)*

For our family's birthday parties, my mother always made these delicious finger-size pites. We looked forward to them almost as much as to our presents. No matter how many she made, there were never enough. These require a more substantial dough, almost like a pizza dough, to hold up to the handling.

FILLING

1½ pounds feta cheese (about 6 cups)

3 large eggs, lightly beaten

2 tablespoons finely chopped fresh dill

Freshly ground black pepper to taste

DOUGH

4 cups all-purpose flour

2 large eggs

½ cup (1 stick) unsalted butter, softened

1 cup warm water

1 egg yolk

To make the filling, combine the cheese, eggs, and dill in a large bowl and mix well. Season with pepper and set aside.

To make the dough, combine the flour, whole eggs, butter, and warm water in a medium bowl. Knead until dough is smooth and elastic. Roll out the dough to a thickness of ¼ inch and cut into triangles, each side about 2 inches long. Place a spoonful of the cheese mixture on each triangle and fold the dough in half. Pinch the edges of the dough together to seal, making sure no filling leaks out.

Preheat the oven to 350° F.

With a pastry brush, coat a large baking sheet with a little melted butter. Place the triangles about ½ inch apart on the baking sheet. In a small bowl, beat the egg yolk with about 1 tablespoon of water and brush this glaze over each triangle. Bake for 30 to 40 minutes, until golden brown. Serve immediately.

MAKES ABOUT 45 TRIANGLES

BOUREKIA ME YIAOURTI (Yogurt Bourek)

Bourek is a Turkish term that means "bite-size appetizer." Although it usually refers to morsels wrapped in fyllo pastry, Yogurt Boureks actually are more like baked dumplings.

3 cups all-purpose flour
1 tablespoon baking powder
¾ cup plain yogurt
1 cup (2 sticks) unsalted butter, softened to room temperature
3 large eggs, plus 2 beaten egg yolks

1 pound kasseri cheese, grated (about 4 cups)
½ cup finely chopped fresh Italian parsley
Salt to taste

Preheat the oven to 350° F.

Sift together the flour and baking powder. Add the yogurt, butter, and 3 whole eggs and knead into a smooth, soft dough. On a floured surface, pat dough out to a thickness of about ½ inch. Cut into finger-size pieces.

Mix the cheese with the parsley and salt, and sprinkle over the top of the dough pieces. Arrange the pieces on a baking sheet about 1 inch apart. Paint the tops with the beaten egg yolks and bake until golden brown, about 20 to 30 minutes. Serve immediately.

MAKES ABOUT 30

MELITZANOSALATA

(Eggplant Salad)

Although we call this dish a salad, it is really more a dip. Two other "salads" of the same sort are Tzatziki *(Yogurt-Cucumber Salad, page 25) and* Taramosalata *(Fish Roe Dip, page 26). Served together with hot pita bread, the three dishes make a wonderful combination of dip appetizers for any party.*

4 large eggplants
1 large onion, finely chopped
   Juice of 1 lemon
1 egg yolk
1 tablespoon red wine vinegar
¾ cup extra-virgin olive oil

1 teaspoon prepared mustard (any kind)
Salt to taste

Calamata olives for garnish

Preheat the oven to 350° F.

Pierce the eggplants in several places with a fork; put them on a baking sheet and bake for about 1½ hours, until the skins start breaking and the eggplants feel soft when pierced with a fork. Remove them from the oven and let cool. Peel the eggplants and chop the pulp finely. Place the pulp in a bowl and add the onion and lemon juice.

In a small bowl, whisk together the egg yolk, vinegar, oil, and mustard and add to the eggplant. Season with salt and stir to combine well. Refrigerate, covered, for at least 1 hour or up to 2 days. Serve cool, garnished with Calamata olives.

SERVES 6

TZATZIKI

(Yogurt-Cucumber Salad)

My mother always had a cheesecloth bag filled with fresh yogurt hanging over the sink in our kitchen. The excess moisture would slowly drain off overnight, and the next day the yogurt—thick and smooth, almost like cream cheese—was ready to use.

16 ounces plain yogurt
2 large cucumbers, peeled and coarsely chopped
4 garlic cloves, minced or pressed
5 tablespoons extra-virgin olive oil

2 tablespoons red wine vinegar
Salt to taste

Finely chopped fresh dill for garnish

Line a colander with cheesecloth and put the yogurt in it to drain overnight. The next day, mix the yogurt with the cucumbers and garlic in a small bowl. Add the oil and vinegar alternately, stirring until the mixture is thick and smooth. Season with salt and refrigerate, covered, for at least 1 hour or up to 2 days, before serving. Serve cool, garnished with dill.

SERVES 6

TARAMOSALATA

(Fish Roe Dip)

I have always loved the salty taste and smooth texture of this dip, which is one of the most popular in the Greek repertoire. Over the years I have collected recipes for many different versions. Some people like their Taramosalata with a bit of texture; others like me prefer it smooth as mayonnaise. Here is my favorite version, which, like a good mayonnaise, requires a quantity of high-quality olive oil to achieve the desired smoothness. The roe used to be obtained from the local gray mullet, but now usually comes from North Sea cod.

8 slices firm white bread, at least 2 days old	5 tablespoons fresh lemon juice
⅓ cup *tarama* (salt cod roe)	2 cups extra-virgin olive oil
¼ cup finely minced onion	Calamata olives for garnish

Soak the bread in water and then squeeze all the moisture out. In a blender or food processor fitted with a metal blade, mix the *tarama*, onion, and 3 tablespoons of the lemon juice until smooth. With the machine on slow speed, alternately add the bread, remaining lemon juice, and oil until the mixture is thick and smooth. The *Taramosalata* may be served immediately or can be kept in the refrigerator for up to 1 week. Serve garnished with Calamata olives.

SERVES 6

SKORDALIA

(Garlic Dip)

When my aunt Vita from Volos made Skordalia, *the smell of garlic would hang in the air for days. A few days before she wanted to make this dip, she would set aside the bread, so that it would be stale enough. On the day of preparation, she would get down her* gouthi, *a deep narrow wooden bowl, and place a heaping handful of garlic cloves in it. She would mash them with a wooden mallet, then add vinegar, oil, and bread, beating very, very fast. Nowadays, I find that my blender does just as good a job. I also use only half as much garlic as Aunt Vita did, which makes the* Skordalia *lighter. Vita always served the dip with fried eggplant or zucchini, but I prefer it with grilled fish, sliced tomatoes and cucumbers, and crusty bread.*

¾ pound firm white bread (about 10 slices), at least 2 days old
5 garlic cloves, pressed

¾ cup extra-virgin olive oil
3 tablespoons red wine vinegar
Salt to taste

Dip the bread into water and then squeeze out all the moisture. In a blender, combine the garlic with one-third of the bread, one-third of the oil, and one-third of the vinegar. Blend at low speed until smooth. Add another one-third of the bread, oil, and vinegar and blend until smooth. Add the remaining ingredients, including salt, blend well, and transfer to a bowl. Cover and refrigerate for 1 hour before serving. (*Skordalia* will keep, covered and refrigerated, for up to 3 days.) Serve cool.

SERVES 6

GARITHES YOUVETSI *(Shrimp with Tomatoes)*

I think the best version of this dish is served in a taverna in Passalimanie, an area of Piraeus famous for its seafood delicacies. Though this is usually served as an appetizer—in small portions with crusty bread—it makes a delicious main course served over orzo pasta.

3 tablespoons pure olive oil
2 garlic cloves, crushed
2 large ripe tomatoes, peeled, seeded, and coarsely chopped
1 tablespoon finely chopped fresh basil
2 tablespoons dry white wine

Salt and freshly ground black pepper to taste
10 large shrimp, peeled and deveined
3 ounces feta cheese, crumbled (a little less than 1 cup)

In a large, heavy skillet, heat the oil and quickly sauté the garlic for 1 minute, without browning. Add tomatoes and sauté for 2 minutes, until soft. Add the basil, wine, salt and pepper, and shrimp. Simmer for 5 minutes, uncovered, over medium heat until the shrimp turn pink. Add the feta cheese. Mix gently and serve immediately.

SERVES 6

KARAVITHES ATMOU *(Steamed Langostino)*

Langostino are also known as prawns, and can usually be found in good fish markets. However, if they are unavailable, you can substitute the largest shrimp you can find. These are cooked in their shells to enhance the flavor, and served in the shells, too.

2 pounds fresh langostino
¾ cup pure olive oil
Juice of 2 lemons

Salt to taste
1 bunch fresh Italian parsley, coarsely chopped

Steam the langostino over boiling water for about 10 minutes, until they turn bright red.

In a small bowl, combine the oil with the lemon juice, salt, and parsley. Serve the langostino warm on a platter, with the dressing on the side for dipping.

SERVES 6

KALAMARAKIA TIGANITA *(Fried Squid)*

During warm spring and summer days, these fried squid are a favorite at outdoor, seaside taverns. To me, nothing seems more quintessentially Mediterranean than these tasty tidbits. Don't shy away from this recipe because of the deep-frying. Remember, Greeks serve this in small portions, along with olives, cheese, or Greek salad, so no one eats more than one or two tiny squid. Use the smallest squid you can find, as they are more tender. Dipping the floured squid quickly into beer before frying is the secret to their crispness. You can also follow this procedure with fresh mussels.

2 pounds fresh small squid (or frozen if fresh is unavailable)	2 cups all-purpose flour
1 teaspoon salt	8 ounces beer, in a bowl
2 cups corn oil for frying	Lemon wedges for garnish

Clean the insides of the squid, then wash thoroughly. Salt them and let them drain in a colander for a few minutes.

In a large frying pan, heat the oil until very hot but not smoking. Coat each piece of squid with flour and dip it quickly in the beer before placing it in the hot oil. Fry the pieces over medium heat until they are crisp and light brown, about 8 minutes. Serve immediately on a platter, garnished with lemon wedges.

SERVES 6

MYTHIA PLAKI

(Mussel Stew)

Tony, a tailor born and raised in Constantinople, is a good friend and frequent visitor to my restaurant. Every time he goes through the kitchen and sees me cooking, he comments wryly, "Don't be cheap with the onions. Put some more in there. Lots of onions and garlic, extra-virgin olive oil—the secrets of success!"

Tony gave me this recipe, a classic among Greeks from Constantinople. It is served at room temperature, with plenty of bread.

½ cup pure olive oil
1 large onion, finely chopped
2 garlic cloves, pressed
1 large carrot, peeled and cut into medium slices
2 large potatoes, peeled and cut into small cubes
3 medium ripe tomatoes, peeled, seeded, and diced

Salt and freshly ground black pepper to taste
2 tablespoons finely chopped celery leaves
3 tablespoons finely chopped fresh Italian parsley
1 cup water
15 large mussels, removed from shells

In a heavy skillet, heat the oil and lightly sauté the onion and garlic until translucent. Add the carrot, potatoes, and tomatoes. Simmer, uncovered, over low heat for 5 minutes, or until the mixture looks like a thick sauce. Season with salt and pepper. Add the celery leaves, parsley, and water. Return to a simmer and cook, covered, over medium-low heat until the carrot and potatoes are soft, about 20 minutes.

Add the mussels to the skillet and simmer, covered, over low heat, for another 10 minutes until the mussels are cooked and the sauce is quite thick. Serve immediately or at room temperature.

SERVES 6

MYTHIA DOLMA

(Stuffed Mussels)

This is another dish from Tony. The allspice, cumin, and cinnamon hint at its Turkish origin.

18 large mussels, in the shell
⅓ cup pure olive oil
1 large onion, finely chopped
1 cup long-grain white rice
2 tablespoons pine nuts
¼ teaspoon ground cinnamon
½ teaspoon ground allspice
½ teaspoon ground cumin

2½ cups water
2 medium ripe tomatoes, peeled, seeded, and diced
Salt to taste
4 tablespoons finely chopped fresh Italian parsley

Lemon wedges for garnish

Scrub the mussels thoroughly and remove beards with a knife. Rinse in cool water. Set aside.

In a large, heavy skillet, heat the oil and lightly sauté the onion until translucent. Add the rice, pine nuts, and spices. Pour in the water and simmer, covered, over low heat, about 15 to 20 minutes, until most of the water is absorbed. Mix in the mussels, tomatoes, salt, and parsley. Simmer, covered, over low heat until all the liquid has been absorbed. The heat will cause the mussel shells to open; the rice mixture will then fill, or "stuff," the open shells. Turn off the heat and allow to cool for about 10 minutes.

Arrange the rice and mussels on a large platter and serve warm, garnished with lemon wedges.

SERVES 6

HTAPOTHI LATHOXITHO

(Marinated Octopus)

This refreshing, cool dish goes beautifully with Calamata olives, feta cheese, and plenty of crusty bread to mop up the marinade. Use best-quality extra-virgin olive oil for flavor.

1 fresh octopus, 2 to 3 pounds (or frozen if fresh is unavailable)	¾ cup red wine vinegar
	1 tablespoon Dijon mustard
1 cup extra-virgin olive oil	

Put the octopus in a medium pot and cover with plenty of warm water. Bring to a boil, cover, and cook over medium heat for about 1½ hours, or until tender. Drain and let cool. Cut into medium pieces and put into a bowl.

In a small bowl, whisk together the oil, vinegar, and mustard. Pour the mixture over the octopus, cover, and refrigerate for at least 2 hours before serving. Serve cool.

SERVES 6

METHISMENO HTAPOTHI

(Drunken Octopus)

Octopus is an excellent mezethes, but don't overdo it. It tastes wonderful and refreshing, but it can feel like a stone in your stomach two hours later if you have too much of it. My mother insists that freezing the fresh octopus for a couple of days and then defrosting it, and beating it on a counter or with a wooden mallet, breaks its muscles and makes the octopus more tender and digestible. I still do this when I cook octopus in Greece; octopus available in America does not seem to require tenderizing.

The following recipe, called "Drunken" because of its wine sauce, is the house specialty of a popular beach taverna in Piraeus.

⅓ cup pure olive oil
1 large onion, finely chopped
   Approximately 2 pounds fresh
   octopus (or frozen if fresh is
   unavailable), cut into medium
   pieces

1 cup dry red wine
3 large ripe tomatoes, peeled,
   seeded, and coarsely chopped
   Salt and freshly ground black
   pepper to taste

In a large saucepan or pot, heat the oil over medium heat and sauté the onion until translucent. Add the octopus and continue sautéing, stirring constantly, for about 10 minutes, until the octopus pieces turn white. Pour in the wine and tomatoes, add salt and pepper, and cook for another 5 minutes, until everything is well combined. Stir in about 7 cups of water and simmer over medium-low heat, covered, for about 1½ hours, until octopus is tender and sauce has thickened. Serve warm.

SERVES 6

REGA *(Smoked Herring)*

Smoked herring is especially popular as an appetizer in Greece, but we frequently serve it (or sardines or anchovies) as an accompaniment to bean or lentil soup. With salad and bread, this makes a complete and nourishing meal.

1 large smoked herring
   Extra-virgin olive oil to taste
   Fresh lemon juice to taste

Calamata olives for garnish

Pierce herring with a long fork and cook, turning several times, over the flame of a gas stove burner for about 10 to 15 minutes, until the skin starts peeling. (Or wrap the herring in aluminum foil and place directly on an electric stove burner, set on high heat, for about 8 minutes a side.)

   Peel off the skin, and cut fish into small pieces. Arrange the fish on a plate, pour olive oil over, add lemon juice, and serve, garnished with olives.

SERVES 6

KOLOKYTHOLOULOUTHA YEMISTA

(Stuffed Zucchini Blossoms)

Look for the largest zucchini blossoms available, as they are easier to handle.

18 large zucchini blossoms
1 cup long-grain white rice
3 tablespoons finely chopped
    fresh Italian parsley
3 tablespoons finely chopped
    fresh mint
1 small onion, finely chopped

⅓ cup pure olive oil
1 large ripe tomato, peeled,
    seeded, and coarsely chopped
Salt and freshly ground black
    pepper to taste
¾ cup warm water

Wash the zucchini blossoms gently and drain them. In a small bowl, combine the rice, parsley, mint, and onion. Add the oil, tomato, and salt and pepper and mix well. Using a small teaspoon, stuff the blossoms with the rice mixture. Arrange them one next to the other in a shallow saucepan, add warm water, and cover. Bring to a boil and simmer over low heat until the rice is cooked, about 30 minutes. Serve warm.

SERVES 6

KOLOKYTHOKEFTEDES *(Zucchini Croquettes)*

Accompany with cool and tangy Tzatziki *(Yogurt-Cucumber Salad, page 25).*

2 pounds zucchini, ends
    trimmed, cut into large
    chunks
2 large eggs
1 large onion, finely chopped
1 cup fresh bread crumbs

4 ounces feta cheese, crumbled
    (about 1 cup)
2 tablespoons finely chopped
    fresh Italian parsley
1 cup all-purpose flour
1½ cups corn oil for frying

Boil or steam the zucchini until they are soft. Drain, transfer to a bowl, and mash with a fork. Mix the zucchini with the eggs, onion, bread crumbs, cheese, and parsley. Shape spoonfuls of the mixture into balls and coat with flour. Heat the oil in a skillet until hot but not smoking and fry zucchini balls in batches over medium heat until crisp and golden, about 5 to 10 minutes. Serve hot.

MAKES ABOUT 30 CROQUETTES

FASOLIA GIGANDES *(Butter Bean Stew)*

This flavorful stew is especially popular during Lent. My mother would place a small bowl of it in the middle of the table along with sliced tomatoes, Calamata olives, Taramosalata *(Fish Roe Dip, page 26), and freshly baked bread to make a healthy and delicious start to a meal.*

1½ pounds dried butter beans (large lima beans)	¾ cup tomato sauce
½ cup pure olive oil	3 tablespoons finely chopped fresh Italian parsley
2 medium onions, finely chopped	Salt and freshly ground black pepper to taste
1 garlic clove, pressed	2 cups water
3 large ripe tomatoes, peeled, seeded, and diced	

Put the beans in a large pot and cover with water. Bring to a boil over medium heat and cook, partly covered, for about 1 hour, or until beans are almost tender. Drain and set aside.

Preheat the oven to 400° F.

In a heavy saucepan, heat the oil and sauté the onions until translucent. Add the garlic, tomatoes, tomato sauce, parsley, salt and pepper, and water. Simmer, covered, over low heat for about 20 minutes, until sauce starts to thicken. Transfer the beans to a casserole or baking dish, pour the tomato mixture over, and stir. Bake for about 40 minutes, until the beans are tender and the sauce is thick. Serve warm or at room temperature.

SERVES 6

STRAPATSATHA *(Omelet Picante)*

A Macedonian specialty, this egg dish is closely related to the Spanish huevos rancheros *and the Italian* frittata.

4 tablespoons pure olive oil
1 small sweet green pepper, finely
  chopped
½ medium sweet red pepper,
  finely chopped
1 garlic clove, pressed
2 ripe small tomatoes, peeled,
  seeded, and mashed

2 tablespoons finely chopped fresh
  Italian parsley
Pinch of sugar
Salt and freshly ground black
  pepper to taste
4 large eggs

In a large skillet, heat the oil and sauté the peppers over medium heat until soft, about 5 minutes. Combine the garlic, tomatoes, parsley, sugar, and salt and add to the skillet. Cook for another 5 to 10 minutes, until the mixture thickens. Season with ground pepper.

Beat the eggs in a small bowl. Stir them into the tomato mixture in the skillet. Cover and cook over medium heat for about 3 minutes, until the eggs are set. Slide the omelet out whole onto a large serving platter and serve hot.

SERVES 6

SAGANAKI *(Cheese Fritters)*

The following recipes make two different kinds of fritters. The first version, which is the classic fritter served throughout Greece, is simply a chunk of cheese coated in flour and fried until crisp on the outside and soft on the inside. The second version, from my region, is a little more involved and results in more of a cheese pancake. Both are flamed at the table to provide extra crispness and flavor, not to mention drama. These fritters are rich, but Greeks eat them in tiny portions, served with other tidbits, as appetizers. They are good with a strong red wine.

8 ounces kefalograviera, kefalotiri, Romano, or any hard, salty yellow cheese (about 2 cups)
1 cup all-purpose flour
3 tablespoons butter, or ⅓ cup olive oil

Ouzo or brandy to flame the dish, warmed

Lemon wedges for garnish

Cut the cheese into slices about ⅓ inch thick. Coat the slices with flour.

In a large, nonstick skillet, heat butter or oil and fry the slices until both sides are golden brown and crisp, and cheese starts to melt. Place them on a heatproof platter, drizzle with warm ouzo or brandy, and ignite. When the flames die down, serve immediately, garnished with lemon wedges.

SERVES 6

SAGANAKI *(Version 2)*

6 ounces feta cheese, crumbled (just under 1 cup)
2 ounces kefalotiri cheese, shredded (about 3 tablespoons)
3 ounces kasseri cheese, shredded (about ⅓ cup)
2 large eggs
Freshly ground black pepper to taste

¾ cup all-purpose flour, plus extra for dredging
2 tablespoons (¼ stick) butter, or ¼ cup olive oil
Ouzo or brandy to flame the dish, warmed

Lemon wedges for garnish

In a medium bowl, mix cheeses, eggs, and pepper until smooth. Add flour and knead dough with your fingers until smooth and firm. Divide in thirds and shape into ½-inch-thick patties. Dredge in flour.

In a nonstick skillet, melt butter or oil and fry patties over medium heat for 3 to 5 minutes on each side, until golden brown and crisp. Place on a heatproof platter, drizzle with warm ouzo or brandy, and ignite. When the flames die down, garnish with lemon, and serve immediately, cut in wedges.

SERVES 6

Soups

(Soupa)

As a child in Karditsa, I used to walk home from school for the midday meal and smell all kinds of wonderful aromas as I made my way through my neighborhood. With just a few sniffs, I could tell exactly what my friends' mothers were preparing, and that made me all the more eager to get home and see what my mother had in store for us. Lunch—usually served around 2:00 P.M.—is almost a holy time for Greek families because it is when everyone gathers to enjoy what has been cooked from scratch all morning, and to catch up on the events of the day.

I always had high hopes for lunch, except on those days when I would round my corner to be greeted by the pungent smell of lemony fish soup or the heavy scent of lentil soup. Like most Greek children, I didn't like soup very much. It was not until I was a college student in Thessaloniki, with its brisk, cool climate in winter, that I came to appreciate warm, filling soups. The many fragrant varieties served in that region enticed me so much that soup became one of my favorite dishes.

Homemade Greek soups, such as the lemony Avgolemono, are sometimes served as first courses, but more often, especially in winter, the more substantial soups are served as main courses, always accompanied by bread and little tidbits such as cheese and olives. On meatless Lent days, my mother often served ospria (many types of dried bean soup), along with olives, anchovies, or smoked herring bathed in olive oil and lemon juice, and a salad of lettuce with green onions and dill.

Now that I have learned to appreciate the wonderful soups I grew up with, I am happy to share them, as well as the best ones I have tasted traveling through different parts of my country. Greek soups have been influenced by many other cultures; some of my favorite soup recipes have come from my friends in Asia Minor. And Greek soups have influenced other cultures in turn, inspiring at least one of the most famous dishes in the world, as you will see when you read the recipe for Kakavia (page 47).

YOUVARLAKIA SOUPA

(Meatball Soup)

With its little meatballs swimming in rich egg-lemon broth, this soup is always a big hit with children. On windy winter nights, my mother would serve it as a meal in itself, accompanied by salad and crisp bread.

½ pound lean ground beef
½ pound lean ground lamb
1 medium onion, finely chopped
¼ cup long-grain white rice
2 tablespoons finely chopped fresh
   Italian parsley
3 large eggs
  Salt and freshly ground black
   pepper to taste

9 cups water
  All-purpose flour for dredging
  Juice of 2 lemons

  Coarsely chopped fresh Italian
   parsley for garnish

In a large bowl, combine the beef, lamb, onion, rice, parsley, 1 egg, and salt and pepper. Mix thoroughly. Pinch off walnut-size pieces of the mixture and roll them into balls.

In a large pot, bring water to a boil. Roll the meatballs in the flour and then carefully lower them into the boiling water. Reduce heat to low, and simmer, covered, for 40 minutes, until meatballs are cooked. Remove from heat.

Beat the remaining eggs and lemon juice in a bowl until frothy. Stir about a half cup of the hot broth from the meatballs into the egg mixture to warm it. Then pour the mixture into the soup pot, stirring constantly. The broth should turn yellow and creamy. Serve immediately, garnished with chopped parsley.

SERVES 6

NOTE: To reheat this soup, simmer over very low heat and do not allow it to boil, or the egg will curdle.

AVGOLEMONO SOUPA

(Chicken Soup with Egg and Lemon)

Avgolemono *is perhaps the most typical of Greek soups. Greeks think of it the way others think of chicken soup—as a remedy for any ailment. In fact, when winter arrived in my hometown of Karditsa, we would often make a very basic version of this soup just to ward off colds. We'd simply sprinkle fresh lemon juice and salt over hot, meaty chicken broth and have lunch and "medicine" all in one.*

True avgolemono—*made with rice or orzo pasta—is also quick and simple to prepare.* Avgolemono *makes a perfect light lunch or elegant first course for a dinner party.*

1 medium chicken (about 3
    pounds)
1 large onion, cut in half
1 cup long-grain white rice or orzo
    pasta

3 large eggs
Juice of 2 lemons
Salt and freshly ground black
    pepper to taste

Wash the chicken well and remove excess fat. Put it into a large pot, along with the onion. Add water to cover. Simmer over low heat, partly covered, for about 1½ hours, or until the chicken is tender. Remove the chicken and onion from the broth and set aside. (You can dice some of the chicken to add to the soup, if you like, or serve the chicken sliced on the side.)

Measure the broth, and if necessary, add water to make 7 cups of liquid. Bring the broth to a boil and add the rice or orzo pasta. Cook, partly covered, over medium-low heat for about 15 minutes, or until the rice is cooked. Remove from heat.

In a medium bowl, beat the eggs and lemon juice until foamy. Add about 1 cup of the warm broth to heat the eggs and then pour the egg-lemon mixture into the soup, stirring constantly until the soup thickens slightly and turns yellow. Add diced chicken, if you wish. Remove from heat, season with salt and pepper, and serve immediately.

SERVES 6

NOTE: Greek chickens are usually free-range and have a superb flavor and very little excess fat. What little fat they do render when boiled for broth or soup provides essential flavor, I think. However, if you are using a fattier chicken, or are on a fat-restricted diet, feel free to skim the soup while it is cooking, or refrigerate the soup later and remove any fat that may harden and rise to the top.

In reheating this soup, use very low heat and do not allow it to come to a boil, as the egg-lemon mixture will curdle.

SOUPA FAKES *(Lentil Soup)*

This substantial soup, usually served with anchovies, pickles, and freshly baked bread, makes a full meal. Meatless, it is thought of as a Lenten soup, served before Easter, or on Wednesdays and Fridays, considered by the Greek Church to be fasting days.

1 pound dried lentils	2 bay leaves
6 cups water	½ cup pure olive oil
2 medium onions, finely chopped	Salt and freshly ground black
2 garlic cloves, minced	pepper to taste
2 large ripe tomatoes, thickly sliced	½ cup red wine vinegar

Pick over the lentils and wash them well. Place them in a pot with water and bring to a boil. Simmer over medium-low heat for about 45 minutes, or until lentils are almost tender.

Add the onions, garlic, tomatoes, bay leaves, oil, and salt and pepper. Simmer the soup, partly covered, over low heat for about 50 minutes, until it has thickened. Stir in the vinegar and heat thoroughly. (Greeks always leave the bay leaves in their cooked dishes, but if you prefer, you may remove them at this point.) Serve hot or warm.

SERVES 6

FASOLATHA

(Lima Bean Soup)

This is another substantial soup with an old history, considered by many to be the national dish of Greece. A winter staple, it has always been a particular favorite on the windy plains and in the mountains of the mainland, where beans are one of the few crops that thrive. Winter, however, is not the only season for hearty bean soups in Greece. Because beans are so nutritious and readily available, these soups are often served year-round. On hotter days, Greeks prefer to eat their bean soups warm or even at room temperature.

1 pound dried lima beans
3 quarts plus 3 cups hot water
2 medium carrots, sliced
2 medium onions, coarsely chopped
2 medium ripe tomatoes, coarsely chopped
2 medium celery stalks, including tops, coarsely chopped
½ cup pure olive oil
Salt and freshly ground black pepper to taste
Fresh lemon juice to taste

Wash and pick over the beans. Place them in a pot with cold water to cover, bring to a boil, and simmer them until their skins soften and wrinkle, about 45 minutes. Drain and add hot water, then add the carrots, onions, tomatoes, and celery. Simmer over medium-low heat, partly covered, for 45 minutes, or until the beans are almost tender and the soup starts to thicken. Add the oil, season with salt and pepper, and cook for another 45 minutes, until the beans are fully cooked and soup has thickened.

Serve hot or warm, sprinkled with a little lemon juice.

SERVES 6 TO 8

Fava Soupa

(Split-Pea Soup)

Santorini, a large island in the Aegean, is just as famous for its processing of split peas as it is for its seafood. Of course, the residents specialize in split-pea soup.

1 pound split peas, green or
    yellow
10 cups cold water
1 large onion, finely chopped
1 medium carrot, coarsely
    chopped
1 medium potato, peeled and
    coarsely chopped

1 large zucchini, peeled and
    coarsely chopped
⅓ cup pure olive oil
    Salt to taste
    Fresh lemon juice to taste

Pick over and wash the split peas. Put cold water in a large pot and add the peas, onion, carrot, potato, and zucchini. Bring to a boil, then reduce heat to medium-low and simmer, partly covered, until vegetables and peas are almost tender, about 1 hour. Stir occasionally.

Add the olive oil and simmer over low heat for another 30 minutes, until soup is thick.

Season with salt and lemon juice. Serve hot or warm.

SERVES 6

Psarosoupa Avgolemono

(Egg-Lemon Fish Soup)

Just as we on the mainland make our Avgolemono *with chicken, people on the coast and on the islands use fish. The technique for both versions is similar.*

10 cups water
3 pounds rock cod, halibut, sea bass, or any firm fish, skinned, cleaned, and cut into big pieces
1 large onion, coarsely chopped
1 large carrot, peeled and coarsely chopped
1 medium celery stalk, with top and leaves, coarsely chopped

1 bay leaf
3 tablespoons pure olive oil
½ cup long-grain white rice
3 large eggs
Juice of 2 lemons
Salt and freshly ground black pepper to taste

Chopped fresh Italian parsley for garnish (optional)

In a large pot, bring water to a boil. Carefully add the fish, vegetables, bay leaf, and olive oil and simmer over medium-low heat for 30 minutes, or until the fish is tender. Remove the fish from the broth and set aside. Continue cooking the vegetables for 10 more minutes, or until tender. Remove the vegetables from the broth, discard the bay leaf, and puree the vegetables, along with a little broth, in a blender or food processor. Set aside.

Strain broth to remove any fish bones. Return broth to the pot and bring to a boil. Add the vegetable puree and the rice. Cook, partly covered, over medium heat for about 20 minutes, or until the rice is cooked. Remove from heat.

In a medium bowl, beat the eggs and lemon juice until foamy and add about 1 cup of the warm broth to heat the eggs. Pour the egg-lemon mixture into the pot, stirring constantly, until the soup thickens slightly and turns yellow. Return the fish pieces to the pot. Season with salt and pepper and sprinkle with chopped parsley, if desired. Serve immediately.

SERVES 6

NOTE: In reheating this soup, use very low heat and do not allow it to boil, as the egg-lemon mixture will curdle.

KAKAVIA *(Fish and Fresh Vegetable Soup)*

Hundreds of years ago, Greek colonizers brought this dish with them to France, where it was transformed into bouillabaisse. In Greece, this soup typically is made with whatever very small fish are left in the nets at the end of a day's fishing.

3 tablespoons pure olive oil

½ medium onion, coarsely chopped

2 green onions, green and white parts finely chopped

½ medium sweet green pepper, seeded, ribbed, and coarsely chopped

1 garlic clove, minced

¼ cup dry white wine

2 medium ripe tomatoes, peeled, seeded, and coarsely chopped

1 medium baking potato, peeled and cut into medium cubes

1 medium carrot, coarsely chopped

1 medium celery stalk, including leaves, coarsely chopped

1 tablespoon tomato paste

2 bay leaves

½ teaspoon crumbled dried thyme

3 cups water

1 red snapper fillet (6 to 8 ounces), cut into small chunks

1 sea bass fillet (6 to 8 ounces), cut into small chunks

8 medium shrimp, peeled and deveined

¼ cup finely chopped fresh Italian parsley

⅛ teaspoon cayenne pepper

Salt to taste

Fresh lemon juice to taste

Heat the olive oil in a large, heavy saucepan over medium-low heat. Add the onions, green pepper, and garlic and cook, stirring occasionally, until softened, about 10 minutes. Add the wine and cook for 1 minute. Stir in tomatoes, potato, carrot, celery, tomato paste, bay leaves, and thyme.

Add the water and bring to a boil. Reduce heat to medium and cook until vegetables are almost tender, about 15 minutes. Add the fish and shrimp, and simmer gently over low heat just until the fish is opaque and the shrimp turn pink, about 2 minutes. Do not overcook.

Add the parsley and cayenne. Add salt and lemon juice to taste. (Greeks always leave the bay leaves in their cooked dishes, but if you prefer, you may remove them at this point.) Serve immediately.

SERVES 6

TRAHANAS SOUPA

(Sourdough Nugget Soup)

One of my fondest memories is of my aunt Vita in Volos making trahanas, *the dried sourdough nuggets that are the basis of this soup. She would start with the freshest eggs and goat's milk, then roll out the dough and cut it into hundreds of strands. She and any helpers she could enlist would spread the strands on clean linen sheets that soon covered every spare bed and available surface in the house. Each day the strands dried a little more, until they could be crumbled into the little nuggets.*

Hardly anyone these days goes to the trouble of making trahanas *nuggets at home. They are usually available in Greek or Middle Eastern specialty stores.*

7 cups beef broth
1 cup tomato sauce
1½ cups *trahanas*
1 tablespoon unsalted butter
   Salt and freshly ground black
     pepper to taste

Grated kefalotiri cheese or
   crumbled feta cheese for
   garnish

Combine the beef broth and tomato sauce in a pot and bring to a boil. Add *trahanas* and simmer over medium heat for 30 minutes, until the nuggets are soft and the soup thickens. Add butter, salt, and pepper, and stir. Serve the soup immediately, garnished with grated or crumbled cheese.

SERVES 6

PATZAROSOUPA

(Beet Soup)

This colorful summer soup, served warm or cold, was the specialty of a popular Thessaloniki taverna for many years. A vivid red, it looks especially appealing served in shallow white soup plates, accompanied by bread and salad.

10 cups water

3 large beets, peeled and cut into small cubes

2 medium zucchini, peeled and cut into small cubes

2 medium potatoes, peeled and cut into small cubes

2 medium onions, coarsely chopped

5 tablespoons unsalted butter

½ cup tomato sauce

2 cups plain yogurt

Juice of 2 lemons

Salt and freshly ground black pepper to taste

In a large pot, bring the water to a boil. Add the beets, zucchini, and potatoes, and simmer over medium-low heat for 20 minutes, until vegetables are almost cooked. Set aside.

In a saucepan, lightly sauté the onions in the butter until golden, about 5 minutes. Stir in the tomato sauce. Pour this mixture into the soup pot and bring to a boil. Reduce heat to medium-low and simmer for 5 minutes, until all vegetables are tender.

In a bowl, beat the yogurt with the lemon juice until smooth and fluffy, then slowly add it to the soup, stirring constantly. Add salt and pepper to taste. Continue cooking over medium-low heat for 1 more minute, until the soup is thick and creamy. Serve warm or cold.

SERVES 6

TANEA SOUPA

(Barley-Yogurt Soup)

My friend Koula gave me this recipe for a tangy, creamy soup from the Pondo region of Asia Minor. People from Pondo have a passion for flavorful cooking, even in simple recipes like this one and the next one.

5 cups water
5 heaping tablespoons pearl
   barley
Salt to taste
1½ cups plain yogurt

4 tablespoons (½ stick) unsalted
   butter
2 tablespoons chopped fresh
   mint

In a medium pot, bring water and barley to a boil over high heat. Reduce heat to medium-low and simmer, covered, for about 30 minutes, or until barley is cooked. Season with salt.

In a bowl, beat the yogurt with a few tablespoons of the hot barley water to warm the yogurt. Over low heat, add the yogurt to the soup, stirring constantly. The soup should look thick and creamy.

In a small saucepan, melt the butter and sauté the mint over medium-low heat for a couple of minutes.

Ladle the soup into warmed soup bowls and spoon about a tablespoon of the butter-mint mixture in the center of each serving. Serve the soup warm.

SERVES 6

TARATORI SOUPA

(Summer Cucumber-Yogurt Soup)

On hot summer nights people from the Pondo region will often serve this refreshing cold soup for a late supper, accompanied by salad and bread. Traditionally they will spoon a few ice cubes into the chilled soup just before serving, to make it as cold as possible, but this is optional.

2 medium cucumbers, peeled
   and coarsely chopped
2 garlic cloves, crushed
2½ cups plain yogurt
1 cup buttermilk
   Salt to taste
3 tablespoons extra-virgin olive
   oil

1 tablespoon red wine vinegar
1 tablespoon chopped fresh mint

Chopped fresh mint leaves for
   garnish

In a large bowl, combine the cucumbers, garlic, and yogurt. Add the butter-milk and salt, mixing thoroughly. Stir in the olive oil and vinegar. Cover with plastic wrap and refrigerate for several hours before serving. Just before serving, add a cup of ice cubes to the bowl, if desired, and sprinkle with mint. Serve cold.

SERVES 6

MAROULOSOUPA

(Lettuce Soup)

A specialty of Norok, a taverna in Athens, this soup is tart and refreshing. Served warm or cold, it makes a perfect summer lunch when accompanied by small plates of olives and cheese or other tidbits.

6 cups water
1 large head romaine lettuce, washed and torn into bite-size pieces
6 green onions, green and white parts coarsely chopped

3 tablespoons unsalted butter
1½ cups plain yogurt
1 tablespoon fresh lemon juice
2 tablespoons chopped fresh dill
Salt to taste

In a large pot, bring the water to a boil. Add the lettuce and cook, covered, over medium heat for about 7 minutes, until lettuce is wilted but not mushy.

Meanwhile, in a small pan, sauté the green onions in the butter for 2 minutes, until translucent. Add the onions to the lettuce and cook for 5 minutes. Let cool.

In a small bowl, beat the yogurt with the lemon juice and dill, and pour it slowly into the soup mixture. Simmer for 2 minutes over low heat, until soup is creamy and thick. Season with salt. Serve warm or cold.

SERVES 6

DOMATOSOUPA

(Tomato Soup)

This soup, like lentil soup, is usually eaten at Lent and on fast days. It's especially popular in the summer, when fresh tomatoes are available. Country and island housewives usually can plenty of their own tomatoes for fall and winter use in recipes such as this, but you can substitute good-quality store-bought canned tomatoes. I have called for orzo pasta in this version, but rice is also often used.

1½ pounds ripe fresh tomatoes (about 4 medium), peeled, seeded, and coarsely chopped; or 1 28-ounce can Italian-style tomatoes

2 medium onions, finely chopped

2 medium celery stalks, including tops, thinly sliced

⅓ cup pure olive oil

1 cup orzo pasta

Salt and freshly ground black pepper to taste

Place the tomatoes, onions, celery, and olive oil in a large pot and add 10 cups of water. (If you are using canned tomatoes, add only 6 cups of water.) Bring to a boil, then reduce heat to medium-low and simmer, partly covered, for about 30 minutes, or until vegetables are almost cooked. Add orzo pasta and simmer, covered, over low heat, for 10 minutes, until pasta is cooked and soup has thickened. Season with salt and pepper. Serve immediately.

SERVES 6

Seafood

(Thalassina)

Karditsa sits in the foothills of the Pindus mountains, three hours away from the seacoast, so fresh fish for us meant pestrofa, or trout, caught in the nearby Peneios River. I remember how the men looked forward to the beginning of trout season in autumn, when they would climb to their favorite fishing spots and spend the day casting their lines for the elusive creatures. We were just as eager to eat the trout, which my mother would usually simply sauté in olive oil and sprinkle with a little lemon juice.

Though we loved our mountain trout, it paled in comparison to the huge variety of fresh seafood we indulged in when we visited our aunt Vita in the coastal town of Volos. Aunt Vita was a particular shopper who always went to the market very early in the morning, to be sure of getting the best selection of the freshest fish. I loved to accompany her on her dawn missions.

As soon as I heard the characteristic squeak of her closet door opening in the morning, I would jump out of bed and throw on my clothes. She was ready and waiting, dressed in a light, airy housecoat and holding a big wallet in one hand and a small net bag in the other.

We would almost fly to the bus stop. We had to get to the psaragora, or fish market, before 7:30 A.M. to catch Kostas, who was "born and raised" in the fish market, according to Aunt Vita. He was always there at 4:00 A.M. chatting with the fishermen who were unloading their daily catch. By 8:00 most of the merchandise had been sold to retailers and Kostas was gone, enjoying his morning coffee in the nearby kaffenion. After consulting with Kostas on the best buys of the day and making a few other stops, Aunt Vita and I headed back home, her net bag bulging with her catch.

Unlike American fish markets, Greek markets do not sell many fillets or steaks. Large fish are rare in the Aegean, with the exception of an occasional red snapper, small swordfish, or tuna. Usually, we buy either medium-size fish such as bream, red mullet, or mackerel, which we grill or bake whole, or small fish such as sardines, small red mullet, white bait, or fresh anchovies, which we pan-fry whole.

In summer, squid (calamari) and octopus sell out as fast as the fishermen can supply them, since Greeks consider fried squid and octopus favorite seasonal appetizers. In the islands, fishermen dry some of their catch in the sun and sell the product in the months when fresh squid and octopus are not available. The dried seafood, plumped up with a warm sauce, is delicious in soups or stews. Luckily, in America squid and octopus are available year-round at larger fish markets; buy small ones, as they are more tender. Larger fish markets also sometimes carry cuttlefish, a cousin of squid. These are slightly larger than squid, with a more elongated body, and are commonly served with a stuffing.

Though different, Maine lobsters are good in any Greek spiny lobster dish. Buy them live, but no more than two pounds each.

The Aegean way of cooking seafood is usually very simple. Therefore, as Aunt Vita knew so well, freshness is the key to flavor. Seek out a large and busy fish market near you and go early, the way Aunt Vita and I did, to get the best selection.

TSIPOURES SCHARA *(Grilled Bream)*

Large fish are rare in the Aegean, so Greeks almost always cook their fish whole, either baking, grilling, or pan-frying them, depending on their size. Island people have a more unusual technique. They often roast a fish over an open fire, placing it in a large, curved, clay roof tile and nestling it in the coals.

6 medium bream, snappers, or porgies (8 to 10 ounces each)	⅓ cup lemon juice
Salt to taste	3 tablespoons finely chopped fresh Italian parsley
½ cup pure olive oil	

Prepare a charcoal fire in the barbecue grill.

Clean the insides of the fish (or have fishmonger do it), wash thoroughly, and pat dry. Sprinkle with salt.

Grill the fish over hot coals until moist and tender when pierced with a fork, about 5 to 8 minutes on each side.

In a small bowl, whisk together the oil, lemon juice, and parsley. Arrange the fish on a platter and pour the dressing over it. Serve hot.

SERVES 6

PESTROFA TIGANITI *(Pan-Fried Trout)*

The simplest treatment is best for fresh mountain trout. Cook quickly over medium-high heat, and turn only once so that the crisp skin stays intact.

6 whole trout (6 to 8 ounces each)	2 tablespoons (¼ stick) unsalted butter, melted
Salt	
2 cups all-purpose flour	
⅓ cup pure olive oil	Lemon wedges for garnish

Clean the insides of the trout (or have fishmonger do it) and wash thoroughly. Pat dry and sprinkle with salt. Dredge the trout in flour and set aside.

Combine the olive oil and melted butter, and heat one-third in a large skillet. Sauté 2 trout at a time over medium-low heat, turning so that both sides brown evenly, about 6 minutes on each side. Turn fish only once to keep skin intact. Remove to a platter and keep warm.

Remove the skillet from the heat and wipe it out with paper towels. Pour in half the remaining butter and oil. (This keeps the butter and flour bits from burning.) Heat the fat, add 2 more trout, and cook as above. Follow this procedure for the remaining trout.

Serve immediately, garnished with lemon wedges.

SERVES 6

GLOSSA TIGANITI *(Fried Sole)*

You can use Dover sole, flounder, or any flat white fish for this recipe.

6 large fillets of sole (6 to 8 ounces each)	2 large eggs
Juice of 1 lemon	1 tablespoon unsalted butter
Salt and freshly ground black pepper to taste	2 tablespoons pure olive oil
1 cup all-purpose flour	Lemon wedges for garnish

Sprinkle the fish with lemon juice and salt and pepper. Put the flour on a large piece of wax paper and dredge the fish, coating thoroughly.

In a wide shallow bowl, beat the eggs. Dip each fillet in the eggs and then dredge again in the flour.

In a nonstick skillet large enough to hold all the fillets in one layer, melt the butter and add the olive oil. Sauté the fillets over medium heat for 5 to 10 minutes, until they are crisp and golden on the outside and tender inside. Serve immediately, garnished with lemon wedges.

SERVES 6

PSARI STO LATHOHARTO

(Red Snapper Baked in Foil)

Cooking the fish in a wrapping of foil or wax paper helps retain the juices. You could also use a large bream in this recipe.

1 whole red snapper (about 4 pounds)	Juice of 1 lemon
4 tablespoons pure olive oil	Salt

Clean the inside of the fish (or have fishmonger do it), wash it thoroughly, and pat dry. Rub the fish with the olive oil. Sprinkle with lemon juice and salt.

Preheat the oven to 350° F.

Place the fish on one end of a large piece of foil or wax paper and roll it up into a tight parcel. Place in a baking pan and cook for about 40 minutes. If you used wax paper, it should be browned but not burnt; if you used aluminum foil, you may wish to unwrap the fish carefully and pierce with a fork to test for doneness. The fish is done when it flakes easily. Cut away wrapping and serve fish immediately.

SERVES 6

PSARI PLAKI

(Red Snapper Casserole with Tomatoes and Peppers)

The word plaki *refers to a method of cooking fish that is very popular around the Mediterranean, where there are French, Spanish, and Italian variations of this dish. In Greece, we use either fillets of larger fish such as red snapper, halibut, or mackerel, or whole smaller fish like fresh anchovies.*

6 red snapper fillets (6 to 8 ounces each)
1 tablespoon lemon juice
Salt to taste
⅓ cup pure olive oil
1 large onion, coarsely chopped
2 large garlic cloves, minced
2 large ripe tomatoes, peeled, seeded, and finely chopped
½ cup finely chopped fresh Italian parsley

½ cup dry white wine
6 bay leaves
4 black peppercorns
4 medium potatoes, peeled and cut lengthwise into quarters
2 medium tomatoes, thinly sliced
1 sweet green pepper, thinly sliced

Arrange fish in a large baking pan and sprinkle with lemon juice and salt. Set aside.

Heat olive oil in a large skillet. Add onion and garlic and sauté over medium heat for about 5 minutes, until onion is soft and translucent and garlic is golden. Add chopped tomatoes, parsley, wine, bay leaves, and peppercorns and simmer for about 20 minutes, or until the mixture thickens, stirring occasionally to prevent sticking. (In Greek cooking, the bay leaves and peppercorns are usually left in the finished dish. If you prefer, you could substitute freshly ground black pepper for the peppercorns and remove the bay leaves after baking.)

Preheat the oven to 350° F.

Pour the tomato mixture over the fish. Arrange the potatoes in the pan around the fish, and place the tomato and pepper slices over the top. Bake until the potatoes are tender and the fish is flaky, 20 to 30 minutes.

SERVES 6

BARBOUNIA MARINATA

(Marinated Red Mullet)

The red mullet available in the United States is nice in this recipe, but I have to admit that, for me, the Aegean barbounia is far superior. It captures the aroma of the Aegean, and has the most delicate flavor of all fish.

Fish are seasonal in Greece, so at the beginning of the summer, when only the small barbounia are available, we pan-fry them for excellent mezes. The following recipe is better with the bigger barbounia we catch later in the summer.

6 large mullets (about 6 ounces each)
Salt and freshly ground black pepper to taste
1 cup pure olive oil
½ cup red wine vinegar

Juice of 1 lemon
1 large onion, finely chopped
2 tablespoons chopped fresh Italian parsley
½ teaspoon Dijon mustard

Clean the insides of the fish (or have fishmonger do it), wash thoroughly, and pat dry. Sprinkle with salt and pepper. In a bowl, mix the oil, vinegar, lemon juice, onion, parsley, and mustard. Pour over the fish and marinate for at least 1 hour.

Prepare a fire in the barbecue grill.

Remove the fish from the marinade and grill over medium-hot coals for 5 to 8 minutes on each side, basting occasionally with the marinade, until the fish is flaky when pierced with a fork. Remove from the heat, brush lightly with marinade, and serve immediately.

SERVES 6

SARTHELES FOURNOU

(Baked Fresh Sardines)

Fresh sardines, unlike the tiny canned variety, are usually about five inches long. You can also use fresh anchovies; both are often available at large fish markets. Just as fresh tuna bears little resemblance to canned, fresh sardines and anchovies offer a treat to those accustomed only to the salty, canned variety.

2 pounds fresh sardines	2 tablespoons dried oregano
⅓ cup pure olive oil	Salt and freshly ground black
1 large lemon, thinly sliced	pepper to taste
4 tablespoons finely chopped fresh	3 garlic cloves, cut in half
Italian parsley	

Preheat the oven to 350° F.

Remove the heads of the sardines, clean the insides (or have fishmonger do it), wash thoroughly, and pat dry. In a large baking pan, arrange the sardines in one layer. Pour the olive oil over them and place the lemon slices on top. Sprinkle with parsley, oregano, and salt and pepper. Strew the garlic around the fish. Bake for 20 to 30 minutes, until the fish is flaky when pierced with a fork and the skin turns golden. Serve hot or warm.

SERVES 6

XIFIAS SOUVLAKI

(Swordfish Kebobs)

Swordfish from the Aegean, like their larger brothers from the ocean, are usually sold cut into steaks, rather than whole or filleted. This simple, fresh dish is good served with pilaf and a Greek salad.

2 pounds swordfish, cut into large chunks

2 sweet green peppers, seeded, ribbed, and cut into large pieces

2 medium onions, cut into large chunks

3 ripe large tomatoes, cut into quarters

12 large bay leaves

¾ cup pure olive oil

Juice of 2 lemons

Salt and freshly ground black pepper to taste

Dried oregano to taste

Prepare a charcoal fire in the barbecue grill.

Soak 6 long wooden skewers in water for 5 minutes to prevent burning or use metal skewers. Alternately thread pieces of fish with the vegetables and bay leaves. Replace any bay leaves that break, or simply sandwich the broken pieces between the fish and vegetables.

Grill over medium-hot coals for about 15 minutes, turning on all sides, until fish is flaky but moist and vegetables are soft and slightly browned. Remove skewers to a serving platter and keep warm.

In a small bowl, mix the oil, lemon juice, and salt and pepper. Pour this over the kebobs and sprinkle with oregano. Serve hot.

SERVES 6

GALEOS KOKKINISTOS

(Hound Shark in Red Sauce)

Galeos is a small shark available in the markets in autumn. It is considered a delicacy and prepared in various ways all over Greece. Often it is simply sautéed in olive oil, along with its delicious roe, and served with Skordalia *(Garlic Dip, page 27) and* Horta Vrasta *(Cooked Greens Salad, page 11). My favorite recipe, though, is this one, which I had many years ago in a small fish taverna in Thessaloniki. The fresh tomatoes and garlic perfectly complement the rich flavor of the fish.*

6 hound shark fillets (about 8 ounces each), or any shark or swordfish fillets

4 large potatoes, peeled and cut into quarters

1/3 cup pure olive oil

1 large onion, cut into thin slices

2 garlic cloves, coarsely chopped

4 large ripe tomatoes, peeled, seeded, and finely chopped

Juice of 1 lemon

3 tablespoons finely chopped fresh Italian parsley

3/4 teaspoon dried thyme

Salt and freshly ground black pepper to taste

Preheat the oven to 350° F.

Place the fillets in a large baking pan and arrange the potatoes around them.

In a large skillet, heat the oil and sauté the onion and garlic over low heat until they are soft and golden, 5 to 8 minutes. Add the tomatoes, lemon juice, parsley, and thyme and mix well. Simmer over low heat, uncovered, for about 15 minutes, until the sauce thickens.

Pour the sauce over the fish and potatoes and shake the pan to distribute the sauce evenly. Season with salt and pepper and bake for about 40 minutes, or until fish is flaky but still moist and potatoes are soft. Serve hot or warm.

SERVES 6

KOLIOS

(Mackerel Baked with Tomatoes)

There is an old Greek saying, "Everything to its own season, and the mackerel in August." In the Aegean, August is the time when mackerel is at its best, plump with delicious roe.

6 medium mackerel (about 8
  ounces each)
3 ripe medium tomatoes, peeled,
  seeded, and finely chopped
1 large onion, thinly sliced
1 cup tomato juice

⅓ cup pure olive oil
1 tablespoon dried oregano
3 garlic cloves, minced
  Salt and freshly ground black
    pepper to taste

Preheat the oven to 350° F.

Clean the insides of the fish (or have fishmonger do it) and wash thoroughly. Pat them dry and lay them side by side in a large baking pan. Strew the tomatoes and onion slices on top, and pour the tomato juice and olive oil over them. Sprinkle with oregano, garlic, salt, and pepper.

Bake, uncovered, for about 1 hour, basting occasionally, until fish flakes easily when pierced with a fork. Serve warm.

SERVES 6

BOURTHETO KERKYRAS

(Perch Corfu Style)

In Corfu, this dish traditionally is cooked and served in a large iron skillet. Against the black of the pan the white fish and red tomatoes look colorful and summery. On especially hot days, the dish is often served at room temperature.

⅓ cup pure olive oil
2 medium onions, finely chopped
5 large tomatoes, peeled, seeded, and finely chopped

1 tablespoon paprika
Salt to taste
6 perch fillets (about 8 ounces each)

In a large skillet, heat the oil and sauté the onions over medium heat until they are soft and golden, about 5 minutes. Stir in the tomatoes, paprika, and salt. Simmer over medium-low heat, uncovered, for about 10 minutes, until the sauce starts to thicken. Arrange the fish fillets in the skillet (layer them if the skillet is not large enough to accommodate them side by side). Cook, covered, over medium heat for about 20 minutes, until fish is flaky but still moist. Serve hot.

SERVES 6

KALAMARAKIA YEMISTA

(Squid with Rice and Pine Nut Stuffing)

In the months when fresh squid are available, Greeks use the smaller ones to make delectable, crisp appetizers. Larger squid make wonderful main courses, stuffed with a flavorful filling and baked until tender. If you've never worked with squid before, don't be intimidated. They're a lot easier to clean than fish. Just be sure to rinse them thoroughly inside and out to get rid of any ink.

3 pounds medium-large squid (about 15 to 18)
⅓ cup pure olive oil
1 large onion, finely chopped
¾ cup long-grain white rice
3 tablespoons pine nuts
4 tablespoons finely chopped fresh Italian parsley
½ cup warm water
Salt and freshly ground black pepper to taste
3 large ripe tomatoes, peeled, seeded, and finely chopped

To clean the squid, separate the head from the rest of the body and discard. Remove the insides and the eyes and discard. Wash the squid thoroughly, remove the tentacles, and set the body aside. Cut the tentacles into small pieces.

In a medium skillet, heat half the oil and sauté the onion over medium heat until soft and golden, 5 to 8 minutes. Add the tentacles and sauté for about 3 minutes, until they turn red. Add the rice, pine nuts, parsley, and warm water and mix well. Simmer over low heat, covered, for about 20 minutes, or until water evaporates and rice is half cooked. Season with salt and pepper.

Preheat the oven to 350° F.

With a small teaspoon, stuff the squid with the rice mixture. Lay the squid in a medium baking pan, one next to the other. Strew the tomatoes over the squid and sprinkle them with the remaining half of the oil. Cover and bake for about 1 hour, until squid is tender and rice is fully cooked. Serve hot.

SERVES 6

Soupies me Spanaki

(Cuttlefish with Spinach)

Cuttlefish is a somewhat larger cousin of squid. It has fewer tentacles but more ink sacs, which means it has to be rinsed and drained even more thoroughly. If you have trouble finding cuttlefish, substitute squid.

3 pounds cuttlefish
½ cup pure olive oil
2 large onions, finely chopped
2 garlic cloves, finely minced
   Juice of 1 lemon
   Salt and freshly ground black
     pepper to taste

2 cups warm water
3 pounds fresh spinach, carefully
   washed, stems removed, and
   torn into large pieces
3 tablespoons finely chopped fresh
   dill

Remove and discard the ink sacs and bone from inside the cuttlefish. Discard the eyes. Wash the cuttlefish thoroughly in plenty of water. Cut them into strips and set aside to drain.

In a large saucepan, heat the oil over medium heat and sauté the onions and garlic until soft and golden, about 8 minutes. Stir in the cuttlefish and sauté until browned, about 8 minutes. Add the lemon juice, salt and pepper, and warm water. Stir well and simmer, covered, over low heat for about 1 hour, or until the cuttlefish are tender and half of the liquid has bubbled away. Add the spinach and stir gently. Raise the heat to medium, and cook, partly covered, until most of the liquid has evaporated and spinach is wilted but not mushy. Serve hot or warm, sprinkled with dill.

SERVES 6

Astakos me Dendrolivano

(Lobster with Rosemary Butter)

When I was a child, my uncle Lakis introduced me to lobster at a wonderful beachfront taverna called Remvi, in the Aretsou area of Thessaloniki. The lobster came to the table with the shell opened and the meat inside cut into pieces, bathed in a wonderful herbed-butter sauce.

Since then I have tasted different lobster dishes all over Greece, especially on the islands of Skiathos and Santorini. Nothing has ever come close to the simple yet delicious lobster I had at Remvi.

In Greece, lobsters are not very big—usually between one and three pounds. Pick lobsters that feel heavy for their size; it means denser, tastier meat.

6 live lobsters, about 1 pound each

3 to 4 cups water

6 tablespoons (¾ stick) unsalted butter, melted and clarified (see Note)

Fresh or dried rosemary to taste

Juice of 1 lemon

Salt and freshly ground black pepper to taste

Preheat the oven to 400° F.

Plunge the lobsters, one or two at a time, headfirst into a large pot of rapidly boiling, salted water. Cover and bring back to a boil. Cook about 5 minutes, until shells turn bright red. Remove with tongs.

With a knife or scissors, cut open the shells on the underside of the lobster tail. Arrange lobsters in a large baking pan and pour the water around them. Cover the pan closely with foil. Place the lobsters in the hot oven and steam for about 10 to 15 minutes, until they are fully cooked. When the lobsters are cool enough to handle, remove the meat from the shells and slice thinly.

In a large skillet, heat the clarified butter over medium heat and add the lobster meat and rosemary leaves. Sauté for a few minutes just to warm the lobster meat, then add the lemon juice, salt, and pepper. Shake the skillet to coat all the lobster meat with the butter mixture. Transfer the meat back to the split shells for serving. Serve hot.

SERVES 6

NOTE: To clarify butter, melt it over hot water in a double boiler. Remove from the heat and let stand for a few minutes, allowing the white solids to separate and sink to the bottom of the pan. Carefully pour off the clear liquid (this is the clarified, or "drawn" butter) and discard the white solids.

HTAPOTHI ME MAKARONAKI KOFTO

(Octopus with Elbow Pasta)

My mother always cooked this dish for Lent, using her home-canned tomatoes from the previous summer if fresh ripe ones were not yet available in the markets. The pasta is added to the pot at the end of the recipe, so as it cooks it absorbs the excess liquid—as well as a lot of flavor.

¾ cup pure olive oil

2 medium onions, finely chopped

1 medium octopus (2 to 3 pounds), rinsed, cut into small pieces, and eyes discarded

4 large ripe tomatoes, peeled, seeded, and finely chopped

2 bay leaves

3½ cups water

Salt and freshly ground black pepper to taste

1 pound elbow pasta

In a large pot, heat the oil over medium heat and sauté the onions until soft and golden, about 5 minutes. Add the octopus and stir over medium heat for another 5 minutes, until the flesh turns white and the skin red. Add tomatoes, bay leaves, and 1½ cups of warm water. Cook, covered, over medium-low heat, for about 1 hour, or until the sauce thickens and the octopus is almost tender. Season with salt and pepper.

Add the remaining 2 cups of water and stir in the pasta. Turn heat to medium-high and continue cooking, stirring occasionally, for about 15 minutes, or until pasta is cooked and sauce is thick. Serve hot.

SERVES 6

Poultry and Game Birds

(Poulerika)

In the countryside where I grew up, there was not a single house that did not have a chicken coop, or kotetsi, in the backyard. During the day, many people would let their chickens roam the neighborhood streets, pecking and scratching, as if they didn't belong to anybody. The hens and chicks from each coop would always stick together in their daily wanderings and go home at night to roost. Somehow, no arguments ever broke out among the neighbors as to whose chickens were whose; we could always tell them apart.

The eggs were a different matter. The chickens would lay them under the bushes, in the fields, wherever they roamed. We children considered any eggs we found outside the bounds of a kotetsi fair game. We delighted in searching for them all over the neighborhood—like a daily Easter egg hunt.

I loved eggs so much that my favorite job at home was gathering the eggs in our chicken coop. I loved to pick them up still warm from the nest. I also loved feeding our chickens. Their favorite treat, as I remember, was watermelon rinds. We saved all the leftovers from our meals, and at the end of the day I would happily take them out to the chickens. I always took special care of my "babies"—chicks (and sometimes ducklings) that I had raised indoors in nests I had made near a warm lamp. Needless to say, these special chickens would periodically "disappear," and though I didn't want to admit it, I knew they had become my dinner.

One of my favorite "babies" grew into a rooster so aggressive that we called him Killer. He was like a guard dog, fiercely attacking and pecking any intruder. Finally, after about three years, my mother couldn't stand him any longer and he ended up in the stew pot, much to my dismay.

Chicken was really a mainstay of our diet in Thessalia, but when autumn came we varied that diet with game. As soon as the hunting season arrived, especially in the Peloponnese, Thessalia, and Macedonia where game is plentiful, the men would go off for days at a time into the woods. Lucky sportsmen would bring home wild hens, quail, hare, even wild boar. Nothing warmed up a cool autumn day better than the rich and well-spiced aroma of roasting game. And, of course, it made me happy that none of my "babies" was going to be dinner that day!

KOTOPOULO KOKKINISTO ME BAMIES *(Chicken with Okra)*

Okra, a vegetable rich in vitamins, is very popular in Greece. However, if it's not cooked properly, it can have a somewhat slippery texture. My mother's trick to avoid this was to choose small, light green okra, trim the stems without cutting into the pod, and dip each in red wine vinegar before cooking. If okra is unavailable, green beans can be substituted.

2 pounds fresh whole okra
1 cup red wine vinegar
⅓ cup pure olive oil
1 large chicken (3 to 4 pounds),
   cut into 4 serving portions
1 large onion, finely chopped
1 pound very ripe tomatoes,
   peeled and crushed

4 tablespoons finely chopped
   fresh Italian parsley
1½ cups water
   Salt and freshly ground black
   pepper to taste

Trim off the okra stems without piercing the pod and briefly dip each pod in the vinegar. Place the okra in a large bowl and set aside.

Heat the olive oil in a large pot. Add the chicken and onion and sauté until the chicken is browned and the onion is soft and golden, about 10 minutes. Add the tomatoes, parsley, and water and rock the pot to distribute them evenly. Season with salt and pepper. Cover and simmer over low heat for about 15 minutes, or until some of the liquid evaporates but the sauce does not begin to thicken.

Add the okra, shaking the pan again to cover the pods with sauce. Cover and simmer over medium-low heat for about 40 minutes, or until chicken is tender and sauce is lightly thickened. The okra should be soft but still hold its shape. Serve hot or warm on a platter, pouring sauce on top of okra and chicken.

SERVES 4

Kotopoulo Yemisto me Feta

(Chicken Stuffed with Feta Cheese)

The stuffing in this recipe is delicious—fragrant and creamy. It is also a good stuffing for small Cornish hens.

1 large roasting chicken (about 4 pounds)

½ pound feta cheese, cut into medium cubes

2 garlic cloves, crushed

½ cup pine nuts

1 tablespoon dried oregano

Juice of 2 lemons

½ cup pure olive oil

Salt and freshly ground black pepper to taste

4 large potatoes, peeled and cut into quarters

¾ cup water

Preheat the oven to 350° F.

Wash the chicken thoroughly and pat it dry. In a medium bowl, gently mix the feta cheese, garlic, pine nuts, and oregano. Stuff the chicken with the mixture. You can skewer the cavity closed if you like, but there is no need to. Place the chicken in a roasting pan and pour the lemon juice and olive oil over it. Season the skin with salt and pepper. Arrange the potatoes around the chicken, add the water, and bake for about 1 hour, or until the potatoes are soft and the chicken is golden brown and crisp.

Carve the chicken and serve on plates with potatoes on one side and a spoonful of the creamy stuffing on the other.

SERVES 4 TO 6

Kotopoulo Kokkinisto me Pilafi

(Chicken in Red Sauce with Rice)

Rice and chicken are cooked together here in a savory tomato sauce; as a result, the rice takes on all the delicious flavor of the chicken. In the summer, we use our fresh garden tomatoes to make this, but when they are not available, canned tomatoes will do. Serve with a green salad.

⅓ cup pure olive oil
1 large chicken (about 3½ pounds), cut into 4 serving portions
1 large onion, finely chopped
Salt and freshly ground black pepper to taste

1½ cups tomato sauce
2 large ripe tomatoes, peeled, seeded, and finely chopped
3 cups water
2 cups long-grain white rice

In a large pot, heat the oil and sauté the chicken and onion over medium heat until the chicken is browned and the onion is soft and golden, about 10 minutes. Season with salt and pepper. Add the tomato sauce and tomatoes, and shake the pot to distribute them evenly. Cover and simmer over medium-low heat for about 30 minutes, until the sauce thickens and the chicken is half cooked. (When the thigh is pierced with a fork, the juices will still be red or pink.)

Pour the water into the pot and bring it to a boil. Add the rice and mix gently. Cover and cook over low heat for about 30 minutes, until rice is done and chicken is thoroughly cooked. Serve hot.

SERVES 4

KOTOPOULO MILANEZA

(Chicken Milanese Style)

My aunt Georgia in Volos would prepare this every time I visited because she knew it was my favorite. It is similar to an Italian risotto, served with chicken pieces and topped with a creamy cheese sauce.

1 large chicken (about 4 pounds)
3 tablespoons unsalted butter
3 tablespoons all-purpose flour
6 cups chicken broth
1 cup milk
3 egg yolks, lightly beaten

Salt to taste
Pinch of ground nutmeg
½ cup grated kefalotiri or
   Parmesan cheese
2 cups long-grain white rice

Remove any excess fat from the chicken, place the chicken in a large pot, and cover with water. Bring to a boil and cook, partly covered, over medium heat for about 45 minutes, or until the chicken is tender. Measure out 6 cups of broth from the pot (add a little water if there's not enough broth) and set the chicken aside, covered, to stay warm.

In a large saucepan, melt the butter over medium heat and whisk in the flour. Cook for about 3 minutes, stirring constantly, until the mixture colors lightly. Combine 2 cups of the reserved chicken broth with the milk and pour gradually into the butter mixture, stirring constantly over medium-low heat. When the sauce starts to thicken, whisk in the egg yolks. Do not let the sauce boil or it will curdle. Remove from the heat and stir in the salt, nutmeg, and cheese.

Bring the remaining 4 cups of broth to a boil in a medium saucepan. Stir in the rice and turn down the heat to medium-low. Partly cover the pan and simmer until rice is done, about 20 to 30 minutes.

Cut chicken into serving pieces. Mound the rice on a big serving platter, arrange the chicken on top, and pour the sauce over all. Serve warm.

SERVES 4 TO 6

KOTOPOULO MARINATO STI SCHARA

(Marinated Grilled Chicken)

The first nice spring day brings out the barbecues in Greece. This simple chicken dish is often part of a mixed grill with pork chops or pork sausages.

1 cup pure olive oil
½ cup dry red wine
1 garlic clove, finely minced
1 bay leaf
1 tablespoon dried oregano
   Salt and freshly ground black
     pepper to taste

2 medium chickens (about 3
   pounds each), cut into serving
   pieces

Coarsely chopped fresh Italian
   parsley and lemon wedges for
   garnish

In a large bowl, combine the oil, wine, garlic, bay leaf, oregano, and salt and pepper. Add the chicken and mix well, being sure that all of the chicken is coated with the marinade. Cover and refrigerate overnight (or for at least 2 hours if you are short on time).

Prepare a fire in a barbecue grill. When the coals have burned down to a medium-low heat, remove the chicken from the marinade and grill for about 15 minutes on each side, until the juices run clear and the skin is brown and crisp. Sprinkle with parsley and serve with lemon wedges. Serve hot or warm.

SERVES 6

NOTE: To test the intensity of the fire, gingerly pass the palm of your hand over it after it has burned for about 15 minutes, at about a foot's distance. If it doesn't burn you immediately, the heat is ready.

KOTOPOULO KRASATO

(Chicken in Wine)

Simple and quick, this is a Greek version of coq au vin. *I usually accompany it with crisp fried potatoes, but it is equally tasty with pilaf.*

⅓ cup pure olive oil
6 medium chicken breasts, skin removed
1 cup dry red wine
3 medium carrots, peeled and thinly sliced

½ pound shelled green peas
½ pound pearl onions, peeled
½ cup water
Salt and freshly ground black pepper to taste

Heat the oil in a large, deep skillet. Sauté both sides of the chicken breasts over medium heat until golden brown, about 5 minutes on each side. Pour in the wine and add the vegetables, shaking the skillet to distribute everything evenly. Add the water and season with salt and pepper. Cover and simmer over medium heat for about 30 minutes, or until chicken is tender and moist and some thin sauce is left in the pan. Serve hot.

SERVES 6

KOTOPOULAKIA YEMISTA

(Stuffed Cornish Hens)

It is traditional in Greece to stuff poultry with ground meat—veal or pork— especially around Christmastime. In this recipe, the hens are perched on a bed of vegetables. The water added to the vegetables slowly cooks away, leaving the hens moist and juicy.

6 medium Cornish hens, about 1
    pound each
1 pound ground pork or veal
2 garlic cloves, finely minced
1 teaspoon dried thyme
½ teaspoon dried rosemary
2 tablespoons finely chopped fresh
    Italian parsley
⅓ cup pure olive oil
6 medium carrots, peeled and
    thickly sliced

6 medium leeks, white parts only,
    thickly sliced
Salt and freshly ground black
    pepper to taste

Thick slices of toasted Italian
    bread and Dijon mustard for
    garnish

Wash the Cornish hens and pat dry.

In a large bowl, mix the ground meat, garlic, thyme, rosemary, and parsley. Stuff the hens with the mixture and close the cavities with a trussing needle and kitchen string.

In a large skillet, heat the oil and brown the hens over medium heat, turning them until they are light golden on all sides.

Put the carrots and leeks in a large, wide pot. Add hot water to cover and bring to a boil. Carefully place the hens in the pot and pour in the oil remaining in the skillet. Season with salt and pepper. Cover tightly and simmer over medium-low heat for about 1 hour, or until hens are cooked and vegetables are tender. If all the liquid has evaporated before the hens are done, add a little water.

Place the vegetables on a large platter and lay the hens on top of them. Serve immediately, with toasted Italian bread and mustard on the side.

SERVES 6

GALOPOULA YEMISTI *(Stuffed Turkey)*

The tradition of roasted turkey for Christmas dinner came to Greece, from northern Europe, so it's really the only time there are turkeys in Greek markets.

The traditional Christmas meal, especially in the countryside, is always chicken served with egg-lemon soup and a pita—usually Tyropitakia *(Cheese Triangles, page 22)* or Kreatopita *(Meat Pie, page 139). In my family, however, we always roasted a turkey, which was stuffed with ground meat, pine nuts, and chestnuts, a local specialty in Thessalia. We would buy the chestnuts from the vendors who roasted them on the street corners, or we would boil them at home in salted water. Some people like to add raisins to the stuffing mixture, but I prefer the delicate, sweet taste of the chestnuts alone.*

¾ cup (1½ sticks) unsalted butter	½ cup pine nuts
1 large onion, finely chopped	Pinch of ground cinnamon
2 pounds ground veal or pork	Pinch of ground nutmeg
1 cup dry white wine	¾ cup water
Salt and freshly ground black pepper to taste	1 fresh hen turkey (about 10 to 12 pounds)
8 to 10 large chestnuts, peeled and chopped (see Note)	Juice of 2 lemons
	1 tablespoon Dijon mustard

Melt 2 tablespoons of the butter in a large skillet. Add onion and ground meat, and sauté over medium heat until the onion is soft and golden and the meat is brown, about 10 minutes. Add wine and cook over high heat until it evaporates, about 20 minutes. Season with salt and pepper. Stir in chestnuts, pine nuts, cinnamon, nutmeg, and water, mixing well. Cover and simmer over medium heat until all the liquid has evaporated, about 30 to 40 minutes.

Wash the turkey thoroughly inside and out, and pat dry. Using a large spoon, stuff the cavity with the meat mixture. (Try to use all the stuffing as, unlike bread stuffing, this does not cook well separately; it becomes too dry.) Sew up the cavity and tie the legs together with kitchen string. Place the turkey in a roasting pan and pour about 2 cups of warm water around it.

Preheat the oven to 300° F.

Melt the remaining butter and add the lemon juice and mustard. Using a pastry brush, baste the turkey with half of this mixture. Sprinkle with salt and pepper and cover with aluminum foil. Roast for 3 hours. Uncover and baste with the remaining butter mixture. Turn oven temperature to 400° F. and roast for 1 hour more, uncovered, until juices run clear and the skin is golden brown. Remove the trussing thread and spoon the stuffing into a serving bowl. Serve the turkey with the stuffing on the side, hot or warm.

SERVES 6 TO 8

NOTE: To peel chestnuts, boil them for 30 minutes, then roast them at 400° F. for another 30 minutes. The peels should be easy to remove.

PITSOUNIA KOKKINISTA

(Squab in Tomato Sauce)

Substitute Cornish hens if squab are not available.

6 squab (about 1 pound each)	6 medium ripe tomatoes, peeled
Salt to taste	and cut in half
½ cup pure olive oil	1 teaspoon black peppercorns, or
2 cups dry white wine	more to taste

Season the squab inside and out with salt. Heat the oil in a large pot and sauté the squab over medium heat until they are evenly browned. Add the wine and bring to a boil over high heat. Cook for about 10 minutes, rocking the pot to distribute the wine.

Barely cover the squab with hot water and add the tomatoes. Sprinkle the peppercorns over all (Greeks traditionally leave the whole peppercorns in a rustic dish such as this, but fresh ground pepper may be substituted if you prefer). Cover and cook over medium heat until the squab are tender, the sauce has thickened, and the tomatoes are soft, about 45 minutes. Serve hot, with pilaf or fried potatoes on the side.

SERVES 6

HENA VRASTI

(Goose Stew)

Like a French poule-au-pot, *this dish provides fowl, vegetables, and broth all at the same time. After cooking, the goose is removed from the broth, cut into serving pieces, and placed on a platter, surrounded by the vegetables. Bowls of steaming, well-seasoned broth are served, and each diner has the choice of having the broth as a first course and then eating the goose and vegetables, or combining all of them in a bowl for a hearty soup. Goose tends to be very fatty, so trim all visible fat before cooking and constantly skim the fat from the broth as it cooks.*

1 goose (8 to 10 pounds), skin and all visible fat removed

2 medium onions, cut in half

3 medium carrots, each cut into 3 pieces

3 medium potatoes, peeled and cut in half

½ bunch fresh Italian parsley, coarsely chopped

Leaves from 3 celery stalks

1 cup dry white wine

Salt and freshly ground black pepper to taste

1 teaspoon dried sage

Dijon mustard

Wash the goose, and then pat dry. Place it in a large pot and add enough water to cover three-quarters of the goose. Bring to a boil over medium heat. Add the onions, carrots, potatoes, parsley, celery leaves, wine, salt and pepper, and sage. Stir and simmer, partly covered, over medium heat for about 1½ hours, or until goose is tender.

Cut goose into big pieces and arrange on a platter, surrounded by the vegetables. Heat the broth and skim it. It can be served on the side or reserved for later use as a base for vegetable soup. Serve warm or hot, with Dijon mustard on the side.

SERVES 6 TO 8

ORTYKIA ME PILAFI

(Quail with Pilaf)

If you don't happen to know any hunters willing to bestow wild quail upon you, domestic quail can often be found in large supermarkets or specialty stores.

In Greece, game birds such as quail are often sautéed in olive oil and stewed with tomatoes and garlic as in this recipe. Their rich flavor takes well to strong seasoning. Pilaf is a good side dish here, but crisp fried potatoes are also traditional.

½ cup pure olive oil
2 medium onions, finely chopped
6 quail (about 1 pound each)
3 large ripe tomatoes, peeled, seeded, and finely chopped

2 garlic cloves
Salt and freshly ground black pepper to taste
3 cups hot water
3 cups long-grain white rice

Heat the oil in a large pot. Sauté the onions and the quail over medium heat until onions become soft and golden and the quail brown evenly, about 5 minutes. Add the tomatoes and garlic and stir gently. Season with salt and pepper. Barely cover the quail with hot water and simmer, covered, over medium-low heat, for about 40 minutes, or until quail are almost done and about 2 cups of liquid remain in the pot. Add the hot water to the pot, bring to a boil over medium heat, and add the rice. Stir gently. Cover and simmer over medium heat for about 20 to 30 minutes, or until the rice is cooked and about 1 cup of sauce remains in the bottom of the pot. (If there is a lot of sauce left, uncover the pot and cook over high heat for a few minutes, stirring constantly so rice and quail don't stick to the bottom.)

Arrange quail and rice on a large warmed platter and serve immediately.

SERVES 6

Meat and Game

(Kreas kai Kenegi)

It's impossible to think of Greek food without calling to mind certain signature recipes, such as mousaka, but if there is one dish that conveys the essence of Greek cooking, I think it has to be spit-roasted lamb. A whole lamb, turned slowly for hours over hot coals, is always the centerpiece of the festivities for that most meaningful of Greek holidays, Easter. It's also significant that a ready-to-roast lamb on a spit traditionally is presented as a gift by an engaged man to his fiancée's family.

Lamb may hold pride of place on Greek tables, but to me this is simply evidence of the deep love all Greeks have for meat dishes in general. No celebration would be complete without a meat dish of some sort: Easter has its spit-turned lamb, Christmas calls for roasted pork, while a dinner for guests might be veal.

Nowhere in Greece is meat eaten with more gusto than in my native Thessalia. I think one reason for this can be traced to the influence of the two ethnic groups that predominate in the region, each of which clings proudly to its ancient customs.

The Karagounithes farm the plains, working the earth and raising their livestock with old-fashioned tools and methods. The best beef and pork come from the Karagounithes. The Karagounithes are easy to spot even today, dressed in their traditional coin-dotted head scarves as they sell their goods in the village markets.

The mountain-dwelling Sarakatsanaei have spent centuries refining the breeding of their sheep and goats and herding the flocks over their rocky haunts. Owing to the Sarakatsanaei, roasted kid is a regional delicacy, and their lamb dishes are unparalleled in quality and variety.

Meat remains almost as much a mainstay of Greek cuisine nowadays as it traditionally has been, despite our heightened concerns about cholesterol in the diet. The reason is that Greeks rarely eat meat more than a few times a week. Family meals are often based on fresh local fish or poultry, and of course, the Greek Orthodox Church mandates several entirely meatless days each week. On those occasions, meals usually consist of bean soups or vegetable dishes, served with lots of crusty bread and olives.

So I'll always savor biting into tender, rich morsels of roasted lamb, for example, but I'll do it as I always have—in moderation.

KREAS KAPAMA

(Savory Meat Stew)

Any meat dish that is cooked in tomato sauce, whether with lamb, beef, or veal, is called kapama. *The basic recipe is always the same.*

1 teaspoon salt
½ teaspoon freshly ground black
   pepper
½ cup all-purpose flour
3 pounds boneless lamb, beef, or
   veal for stew (or any
   combination), cut into chunks
⅓ cup pure olive oil

1 large onion, finely chopped
1 cup dry white wine
5 ripe large tomatoes, peeled,
   seeded, and finely chopped
   Pinch of ground cinnamon
1 garlic clove, crushed
   Salt to taste

Combine the salt, pepper, and flour in a large bowl and dredge the meat chunks in the mixture, shaking off any excess. Heat the oil in a large pot and add just enough meat to cover the bottom of the pot without crowding. Sauté over medium heat, turning the chunks so that they will brown evenly. Remove meat to a platter as the chunks brown and continue browning the remainder of the uncooked meat in batches.

In the same pot, sauté the onion until it becomes soft and golden, about 5 minutes. Return the meat to the pot and add the wine, stirring with a wooden spoon to scrape up the brown bits on the bottom of the pot. Add the tomatoes, cinnamon, and garlic; simmer, covered, over medium-low heat until meat is tender, about 1 hour. The sauce should be thick, but if the mixture seems dry before meat is done, add a little water. Adjust salt to taste. Serve hot.

SERVES 6

MOSHARI ME KOLOKYTHIA

(Veal with Zucchini)

To vary the basic kapama *recipe, summer vegetables such as zucchini, okra, eggplant, or green beans are often added; if those are not available, potatoes, rice, orzo, or egg noodles are used.*

⅓ cup pure olive oil

4 pounds boneless veal or beef for stew, cut into chunks

2 medium onions, finely chopped

4 large ripe tomatoes, peeled, seeded, and finely chopped

Salt and freshly ground black pepper to taste

5 tablespoons finely chopped fresh Italian parsley

3 pounds small zucchini, stems trimmed, cut in half

In a large pot, heat the oil and add the meat and onions. Sauté over medium heat, turning meat chunks until they are evenly browned and the onions turn soft and golden, about 8 minutes. Add the tomatoes, salt and pepper, and parsley. Add enough water to half cover the meat. Stir gently. Cover and simmer over medium-low heat for about 45 minutes, or until the meat is almost tender and the liquid has reduced by half.

Place the zucchini on top of the meat and shake the pot so the sauce is evenly distributed. Cover again and cook over medium heat for about 15 minutes, until zucchini are tender and sauce is further reduced. Serve hot or warm.

SERVES 6

PASTITSATHA
(Veal and Pasta)

Corfu, an island in the Ionian Sea, is the part of Greece that is closest, both geographically and spiritually, to Italy. Corfuans even speak Greek with an Italian accent. Pastitsatha, one of their specialties, shows the influence of their neighbors to the west. Notice that in this recipe the meat should be cut not into stew-size chunks, but into six larger serving pieces. This is a common way of serving meat in Greece. The result is like an individual pot roast.

⅓ cup pure olive oil
3 pounds boneless shoulder of veal, divided into 6 big chunks
1 large onion, finely chopped
2 tablespoons red wine vinegar
1 cup dry white wine

5 large, very ripe tomatoes, peeled and crushed
Salt and freshly ground black pepper to taste
1½ pounds spaghetti
4 ounces kefalotiri or Parmesan cheese, grated (about 1 cup)

In a large pot, heat the oil and add the veal and onion. Sauté over medium heat until the meat colors lightly and the onion turns golden, about 8 minutes. Add the vinegar and wine, turn up the heat, and cook until the liquid is reduced by half. Stir in the tomatoes, salt, and pepper. Cover and simmer over medium-low heat until meat is tender and sauce thickens, about 45 minutes.

In a large pot filled with boiling salted water, cook the spaghetti until done. Drain and arrange on a large warmed platter. Remove the veal from the sauce and keep warm. Pour the sauce over the spaghetti, then arrange the veal pieces on top. Sprinkle with the cheese and serve at once.

SERVES 6

MOSHARI SOFRITO *(Veal Sofrito)*

This is a dish you'll eat only in Corfu, where the tavernas serve it as a specialty, with baked or fried potatoes on the side. The tavernas usually make it with the thin veal scaloppine, but you can use a more economical cut if you prefer.

3 pounds boneless veal (scaloppine or stew chunks)	Salt to taste
½ cup all-purpose flour	4 garlic cloves, finely minced
½ cup (1 stick) unsalted butter or olive oil	2 tablespoons red wine vinegar
	1 cup dry white wine
	1 cup hot water

Dredge the veal in the flour and shake off excess. In a large saucepan, melt the butter over medium heat and sauté the veal on all sides, until lightly colored. Season with salt. Add the garlic and sauté for a few more minutes. Pour in the vinegar and wine, stirring and scraping the pan to combine the ingredients, and bring the liquid to a boil. Reduce the heat to medium-low and add the hot water, stirring well. Cover and simmer until meat is tender and a little thin sauce remains in the pan, about 40 minutes. Serve hot.

SERVES 6

PASTITSIO *(Macaroni Pie with Meat Sauce)*

No Greek home (or cookbook, for that matter) would be complete without its version of Pastitsio. The creamy béchamel sauce gives this casserole its characteristic richness—and also makes it much more elegant than any ordinary macaroni casserole. Serve this when you feel the urge for something simple but indulgent.

We usually make this dish with a thick, hollow form of spaghetti called bucatini, but you can use elbow pasta instead. Sometimes I like to add mushrooms sautéed in garlic to the basic meat sauce.

1 pound *bucatini* or elbow pasta
1 tablespoon pure olive oil
1 large onion, finely chopped
1½ pounds lean ground beef
½ cup dry white wine

1½ cups tomato sauce
Pinch of ground cinnamon
Salt and freshly ground black
    pepper to taste

BÉCHAMEL SAUCE

1 cup (2 sticks) unsalted butter
1½ cups all-purpose flour
6 cups milk
4 large eggs, lightly beaten

Salt and freshly ground black
    pepper to taste
12 ounces kefalotiri cheese, grated
    (about 3 cups)

Cook the pasta until al dente in a large kettle of boiling, salted water. Drain and set aside.

In a large saucepan, heat the oil, add the onion and ground beef, and sauté over medium heat until the onion is translucent and the meat is evenly browned, about 5 minutes. Add the wine and turn the heat to high. Cook, stirring constantly so that meat does not stick to pan, for about 2 minutes. Add the tomato sauce, cinnamon, and salt and pepper. Partly cover the pan and simmer over medium heat for about 30 minutes, until the meat sauce thickens. Set aside.

To prepare the sauce, melt the butter in a large saucepan over medium-low heat. Whisk in the flour, stirring constantly until mixture is smooth and golden. Add the milk, a little at a time, whisking vigorously after each addition. Continue stirring until mixture thickens. Off the heat, beat in the eggs, salt and pepper, and half the cheese, stirring until smooth.

Preheat the oven to 350° F.

In a large bowl, thoroughly combine the pasta, meat mixture, and sauce. Butter the bottom of a large (about 12 by 17-inch) baking pan or 2 smaller ones and spread the mixture evenly in it. Sprinkle with the remaining cheese. Bake for 30 to 45 minutes, or until the cheese is golden brown. Let the *Pastitsio* cool slightly before serving so the slices will hold their shape.

SERVES 6 TO 8

SOUVLAKIA

(Meat Kebobs)

Tender pieces of lamb or beef, cut into small chunks, are excellent for grilling on skewers, especially when they are threaded between slices of pepper, tomatoes, and onions. Souvlakia are served in tavernas or grilled at home. Also, there are little stands all over Greece called souvlatzithika, where smaller versions of souvlaki are served: usually pork grilled on bamboo skewers, served with pita bread or slices of country bread, Tzatziki (Yogurt-Cucumber Salad, page 25), and chopped onions on the top.

For this recipe, be sure to choose firm small tomatoes that can withstand the heat of the grill.

3 pounds lean boneless leg of
    lamb or beef round, cut into
    medium cubes
2 large sweet green peppers,
    seeded, ribbed, and cut into
    chunks
2 medium onions, cut into
    quarters

6 firm small tomatoes
½ cup pure olive oil
    Juice of 2 lemons
    Salt and freshly ground black
      pepper to taste
1 tablespoon dried oregano

    Lemon wedges for garnish

Prepare a charcoal fire in the barbecue grill.

Soak 6 long wooden skewers in water for 5 minutes, or use metal skewers. Alternately thread chunks of meat and vegetables on skewers. Mix the olive oil with the lemon juice in a small bowl. Put the skewers on the grill when medium-hot and cook for about 8 minutes total, basting with the olive oil–lemon juice mixture and turning to brown evenly. When done, place the kebobs on a warm platter and season with the salt and pepper and oregano. Serve immediately, garnished with lemon wedges.

SERVES 6

SOUTZOUKAKIA SMYRNEIKA

(Meatballs Baked in the Style of Smyrna)

The original of this recipe was given to me by my friend Lily Alikabiotis, whose family comes from Asia Minor. The spiciness of the dish, with its cumin and green Calamata olives, shows that influence. The traditional method of preparation requires frying the meatballs in oil first, a step I think is unnecessary.

3 slices stale, firm white bread
3 tablespoons finely chopped
    fresh Italian parsley
1½ pounds ground beef or lamb
3 garlic cloves, crushed
1 large egg
⅓ cup pure olive oil
    Salt and freshly ground black
    pepper to taste

2 teaspoons ground cumin, or
    more to taste
4 large ripe tomatoes, peeled and
    crushed
½ cup dry red wine
    Pinch of sugar
½ teaspoon salt
1 cup green Calamata olives
3 large potatoes, peeled and
    quartered

Soak the bread in a small bowl of water for a few seconds and then squeeze it hard to express all the moisture. Crumble or tear it into pieces. In a large bowl, combine bread, parsley, meat, garlic, egg, 2 tablespoons of the olive oil, salt and pepper, and cumin. Knead until ingredients are well blended, then shape into 18 meatballs. Place them in a 9 by 13-inch baking pan.

In a medium bowl, combine the tomatoes, remaining oil, wine, sugar, and the salt. Mix well and pour over the meatballs.

Preheat the oven to 350° F.

Put the olives in a small saucepan, cover with water, and bring to a boil. Simmer, uncovered over medium heat, for about 15 minutes to remove excess saltiness or sourness. Drain and sprinkle the olives between the meatballs in the baking pan. Layer the potato quarters on top. Bake for about 40 minutes, or until the potatoes are soft and the meatballs are browned.

To serve, arrange 3 meatballs on each plate, with potatoes and olives on the side, and pour some of the sauce over all. Serve hot.

SERVES 6

MOUSAKA

An American friend once told me that, from what she knew of Greek food, she thought we ate only mousaka, spanokopita, *and* dolmathes. *I laughed. It's true that these are three of our most popular dishes, but* mousaka *is definitely a dish for special occasions—to please a guest, or for a festive Sunday meal. Furthermore, it's usually made only in the summer, when ripe, sweet eggplant is in season. (However, many people substitute zucchini or, in winter, sliced potatoes when eggplant is not available.)*

Over the years I have tasted dozens of versions of mousaka, *but I still think this recipe, my mother's, is the best. She achieves the perfect balance among the meat, the eggplant, and the creamy béchamel. Though it is rather rich (it is for special occasions, after all), it never feels heavy.*

By the way, don't be alarmed at the large quantity of salt in this recipe. The salt simply removes the bitterness in the eggplant and does not remain in the finished dish. The same is true of the frying oil. At first, eggplant absorbs lots of oil but as it browns and softens, it exudes its liquid, including most of the oil. In my experience, this method results in a less oily finished dish than one in which the eggplant is simply sautéed.

4 large eggplants
¾ cup salt
2 cups corn oil for frying
2 tablespoons pure olive oil
2 medium onions, finely chopped
1½ pounds lean ground beef

¾ cup dry white wine
Salt and freshly ground black
  pepper to taste
Pinch of ground cinnamon
1½ cups tomato sauce

BÉCHAMEL SAUCE
1 cup (2 sticks) unsalted butter
1½ cups all-purpose flour
6 cups milk
4 large eggs, lightly beaten

Salt and freshly ground black
  pepper to taste
1½ cups grated kefalotiri cheese

Wash the eggplants and trim off the stems. Cut them into slices about ⅓ inch thick. Fill a large bowl with about 2½ quarts of water and add the salt. Soak the eggplant slices for about 1 hour to remove any bitterness and excess moisture. (The water will turn brownish.) Drain the slices and pat them dry.

Heat the corn oil in a large skillet. Fry the eggplant slices over medium heat until they are soft and both sides are brown, about 5 minutes. Remove the slices and drain on paper towels. Set aside.

Heat the olive oil in a large saucepan and sauté the onions over medium heat until soft and golden, about 5 minutes. Add the ground beef, turn the heat to high, and continue sautéing until the meat browns evenly. Pour the wine into the saucepan and stir over high heat until it evaporates, about 5 minutes. Season with salt, pepper, and cinnamon. Add the tomato sauce and stir. Simmer, covered, over medium-low heat, stirring frequently, about 30 minutes, until sauce thickens. Set aside.

To make the sauce, melt the butter in a large saucepan over medium heat. Whisk in the flour and continue whisking until smooth. Add the milk a little at a time, whisking vigorously after each addition. Simmer over low heat, stirring constantly, until mixture has thickened. Off the heat, add the eggs, salt and pepper, and half the cheese, stirring until smooth.

Preheat the oven to 400° F.

Layer the eggplant slices in the bottom of a medium (about 10 by 15-inch) rectangular baking pan. Spread the meat sauce evenly over the eggplant. Pour the sauce over the meat layer. Sprinkle with the remaining kefalotiri cheese and bake until the top is golden brown, about 30 to 40 minutes. Serve hot.

SERVES 6 TO 8

VARIATION: **PAPOUTSAKIA** (*Little Shoes*)

This dish uses the same ingredients as the regular *mousaka*, but looks much more elegant since it is served in individual eggplant shells. The only difference in preparation is that instead of slicing the eggplants, you cut them in half lengthwise. With a sharp knife, make slits in the pulp and soak the eggplants in salted water. Drain and fry exactly as in the basic recipe. Arrange the shells on a large baking sheet and stuff with the meat filling. Top with the sauce, sprinkle with cheese, and bake at 400° F. until the eggplant is soft and the top golden brown, about 30 minutes. Serve hot.

SERVES 8

LAHANODOLMATHES

(Stuffed Cabbage)

The tender, curved leaves of green cabbage make a good winter substitute for grape leaves in this version of dolmathes. A large cabbage whose leaves are not too tightly closed is easiest to work with. The Lahanodolmathes can be as big or as small as you wish, depending on the size of the cabbage leaves.

1 large green cabbage (about 4 pounds)
1½ pounds ground beef or lamb
1 large onion, finely chopped
5 tablespoons long-grain white rice
3 tablespoons finely chopped Italian parsley

Salt and freshly ground black pepper to taste
2 tablespoons (¼ stick) unsalted butter
2 tablespoons all-purpose flour
3 cups beef stock
3 egg yolks
Juice of 1 lemon

Bring a large pot of water to a boil and carefully lower the cabbage into it. Blanch it in the boiling water for about 10 minutes, until the leaves are wilted but still hold their shape. Drain the cabbage. When it is cool enough to handle, peel off the leaves one by one, trimming any tough stems. Set the leaves aside.

In a large bowl, combine the meat, onion, rice, parsley, and salt and pepper. Mix well. Lay a cabbage leaf flat and place a full tablespoon of the meat mixture on the widest part of the leaf. Fold up the bottom first, then tuck in the sides and roll the leaf into a tight packet. Proceed until you have used up the meat filling, reserving a few unfilled cabbage leaves and pieces.

Lay the reserved leaves in the bottom of a large, heavy pot and arrange the packets tightly, folded side down, on top. Make several layers of cabbage packets, each layer tightly packed to keep the packets from unfolding. Place a heavy heatproof dish or plate on top and add water just to cover the cabbage packets. Simmer, covered, over medium heat for about 30 to 45 minutes, or until rice is cooked and cabbage is soft but not mushy. Remove packets to a platter and keep warm. Reserve 3 cups of the cooking stock.

In a medium saucepan, melt the butter, add the flour, and whisk until mixture colors lightly. Add the reserved stock and stir constantly over medium-low heat until sauce thickens slightly. In a small bowl, beat the egg yolks with the lemon juice until foamy. Spoon some of the hot sauce into the yolks to warm them and then pour the yolks into the sauce off the heat, stirring constantly to keep it from curdling. Pour the sauce on top of the cabbage rolls. Serve hot or warm.

SERVES 6 TO 8

PAITHAKIA ARNISIA STI SCHARA
(Barbecued Lamb Chops)

In the spring and summer, many tavernas specialize in barbecued lamb chops. Accompany these simple chops with a green salad, bread, and Tzatziki *(Yogurt-Cucumber Salad, page 25).*

3 pounds loin lamb chops	Salt and freshly ground black
Juice of 1 lemon	pepper to taste
½ cup pure olive oil	
3 teaspoons dried oregano	Lemon wedges for garnish

Trim excess fat from lamb chops. Rinse them, pat them dry, and lay them in 1 layer in a large baking pan.

In a small bowl, mix the lemon juice with the oil and 1 teaspoon of the oregano. Pour the mixture over the chops and refrigerate for 3 or 4 hours, turning them periodically.

Prepare a fire in a barbecue grill. When the coals have burned down to medium heat, remove the chops from the marinade and place them on the hot grill. Cook about 5 minutes on each side, basting with the marinade.

In a small bowl, mix the remaining oregano with the salt and pepper. When the chops are done, sprinkle them with the mixture and serve them hot, garnished with lemon wedges.

SERVES 6

ARNAKI EXOHIKO

(Country Baby Lamb, Wrapped in Fyllo)

In this recipe, crisp fyllo pastry encloses tender chunks of baby lamb and a vegetable-herb stuffing. It's called "country" because, in the rural areas of Greece, people could just go out into their well-tended gardens and pick handfuls of fresh vegetables and herbs to add flavor to their cooking.

¼ cup pure olive oil

7 green onions, green and white parts finely chopped

1 leg of baby lamb (about 3 pounds), boned and cut into 6 large chunks

1 pound small round potatoes, peeled

1 pound medium carrots, thickly sliced

12 ounces fresh shelled green peas

3 tablespoons finely chopped fresh dill

Salt and freshly ground black pepper to taste

12 ounces feta cheese, coarsely crumbled (about 3 cups)

1 pound commercial fyllo pastry

½ cup (1 stick) unsalted butter, melted

Heat the oil in a large pot. Sauté the green onions and meat over medium heat until onions are soft and golden and meat is evenly browned, about 10 minutes. Add water barely to cover. Simmer, covered, over medium heat for about 45 minutes, or until meat is almost cooked and the liquid is reduced by half. Add vegetables and dill, and continue cooking over medium heat until meat is tender and just a little liquid is left in the pot, about 45 minutes. Season with salt and pepper. Add the feta cheese and mix gently.

Preheat the oven to 350° F.

Cut each fyllo sheet in half and lay one half on top of the other. With a pastry brush, lightly spread some of the melted butter on the top. Place a piece of meat and some of the vegetable-cheese mixture at the narrow end of the sheet and fold it into a large, square parcel, tucking the ends in tightly as you go. Lay the parcels on a baking sheet, one next to the other. Brush the tops lightly with more melted butter.

Bake for 45 minutes to 1 hour, or until golden brown and crisp. Serve hot.

SERVES 6

NOTE: Fyllo dough is available in one-pound packages in the market. Remaining fyllo can be wrapped in plastic and saved in the freezer.

ARNI STI STAMNA *(Lamb in a Pottery Dish)*

Although most modern Greek cooks use metal cookware, there are still some dishes that taste best when cooked in old-fashioned pottery. Many cookware stores carry glazed pottery baking dishes; look for one about 15 inches long, with a lid. In the old days, a Greek housewife used to seal the lid of her pottery dish with bread dough to keep the juices in, but nowadays it's easier to use aluminum foil.

½ cup pure olive oil
1 leg of baby lamb (5 to 6 pounds), boned and cut into 6 large chunks
Juice of 1 lemon
2 large ripe tomatoes, peeled, seeded, and diced

Salt and freshly ground black pepper to taste
5 ounces kefalotiri or feta cheese, cut into 6 slices
1 tablespoon all-purpose flour
¾ cup dry white wine
½ cup hot water

Heat ¼ cup of the oil in a large, heavy skillet. Sauté the lamb chunks until they are evenly browned. Transfer them to a shallow pottery baking dish large enough to hold all the meat in 1 layer. Sprinkle with lemon juice, spread the diced tomatoes on top, and season with salt and pepper. Place one slice of cheese on each piece of lamb.

Preheat the oven to 400° F.

Heat the remaining oil in the skillet and add the flour. Stir over medium heat for a few minutes, until the mixture is smooth and lightly colored. Turn the heat to low and add the wine and hot water. Stir constantly until the mixture thickens slightly. Pour the sauce over the lamb. Place the cover on the pottery dish and carefully wrap the whole dish in aluminum foil to seal in the moisture. Bake for about 1 hour and 15 minutes. Remove the foil and serve immediately.

SERVES 6

ARNI BOUTI PSITO *(Roasted Leg of Lamb)*

Lamb plays a big role in Greek cooking, but never more so than on Easter Sunday, when a whole, spit-roasted lamb is the centerpiece of the festivities.

In the days before Easter, the entire household goes into a frenzy of spring cleaning and preparation. On Holy Thursday it is traditional to serve Spanokopita (Spinach Pie, page 132) minus the cheese, since it is a time of fasting. On Friday, the only sound to be heard is the mournful ringing of the church bells in the distance. People spend much time in church and no time cooking. In some areas it is traditional to have only Greek coffee with bread; in others they serve lettuce dipped in vinegar or lentil soup seasoned only with vinegar. Holy Saturday brings back all the activity. The Greek housewife gets to work preparing the Easter Eve meal, including an Easter soup and Tsourekia (Easter Sweet Bread, page 172). At midnight, everybody stays up for the service of the Resurrection; candles are lighted from the single altar flame and passed from person to person. Then the lighted candles are brought home from the church, and a cross in smoke is drawn on the top of the front door. Afterward, everyone sits down to enjoy the Easter Eve meal.

The next day, of course, the men get down to the most important part of the feast: the lamb. As they tend the spit in a courtyard or garden, neighbors, friends, and relatives stop by for drinks and mezethes.

A whole, spit-roasted lamb is not something you can easily try at home, but this roast leg of lamb makes a good substitute. As on the spit, the secret here is long and slow cooking. Greeks like their lamb well done, and our butchers will often chop through the leg bones in several places to ensure even cooking and penetration of the garlic and spices.

3 lemons
1 leg of lamb (8 to 10 pounds)
4 garlic cloves, halved
4 large potatoes, peeled and cut into quarters
½ cup pure olive oil

Salt and freshly ground black pepper to taste
3 teaspoons dried oregano, or more to taste
1 cup water

Halve one of the lemons and rub the halves all over the meat. With the point of a sharp knife, cut deep pockets all over the lamb and insert the garlic.

Preheat the oven to 200° F.

Place the lamb in a roasting pan, arrange the potatoes around it and sprinkle with olive oil, salt and pepper, and oregano. Pour water into the pan. Sprinkle the juice of the remaining lemons over the potatoes.

Roast for about 1½ hours, until the skin turns yellow. Turn up the oven heat to 450° F., and roast until skin is golden brown and crisp and juices run clear, about 1 hour more. Serve hot.

SERVES 6

ARNI FRIKASE *(Lamb Fricassee)*

This is a very light lamb stew with greens and the classic Greek egg-lemon sauce. In some areas, artichoke hearts are used instead of greens.

2 medium heads romaine lettuce
2 pounds curly endive
3 pounds boneless shoulder of
    lamb, cut into 6 large chunks
½ cup all-purpose flour
5 tablespoons pure olive oil
2 bunches green onions, green
    and white parts finely chopped

4 tablespoons finely chopped fresh
    dill, or more to taste
Salt and freshly ground black
    pepper to taste
3 large eggs
    Juice of 1 lemon

Discard the dark outer leaves of the lettuce and trim off the stem. Wash and dry the remaining leaves and cut into large pieces. Trim the stems from the endive (leave them whole) and wash and dry them, too. Plunge the lettuce and endive into a large pot of boiling water and blanch for about 2 minutes, until wilted but still firm. Drain and set aside.

Dredge the lamb chunks with flour and shake off any excess. Heat the oil in a large pot. Sauté the lamb until it is evenly browned, turning frequently, about 5 to 10 minutes. Add the green onions and dill, and mix well. Barely cover the lamb with water and cook, covered, over medium heat for about 1 hour, or until meat is almost cooked. Add the lettuce and endive, and mix well. Cover and cook over medium-high heat for 3 to 5 minutes, or until the meat is tender and greens are cooked but not mushy. About 2 cups of liquid should remain in the pot. (If there is more, boil uncovered over high heat to reduce it.) Season with salt and pepper.

In a small bowl, beat the eggs with the lemon juice until foamy. Stir in some of the hot liquid from the pot to warm the eggs. Then pour the egg mixture back into the pot. Turn the heat to low and stir gently to mix in the egg-lemon sauce and allow it to thicken slightly. Do not let it boil or it will curdle. Serve the lamb chunks and greens in deep soup plates like a stew, with the egg-lemon sauce poured on top. Serve hot.

SERVES 6

ARNI KLEFTIKO *(Thief's Lamb)*

There are many romantic stories explaining the origins of this dish, which always features lamb baked in tight paper packets. One version begins in the early 1800s, when the Greeks rebelled against the Turks, who had occupied Greece for 400 years. Outnumbered, the Greeks took to the steep mountains to hide in caves. From there, they conducted raids, fighting the occupiers and stealing their food. Legend has it that wrapping the meat was one of their favorite ways of cooking the purloined lamb, perhaps because the paper parcels kept the delicious smells from reaching the Turks.

4 tablespoons pure olive oil
1 leg of baby lamb (5 to 6 pounds), boned and cut into 6 large chunks
5 green onions, green and white parts coarsely chopped
2 cups plain yogurt

3 tablespoons finely chopped fresh dill
½ teaspoon dried oregano
½ teaspoon dried thyme
Salt and freshly ground black pepper to taste

Heat the oil in a large skillet. Sauté the chunks of lamb until they brown, taking care not to crowd them in the skillet, about 10 minutes. Set the lamb aside. Add the green onions to the skillet and sauté until soft and golden, about 3 minutes. Remove the skillet from the heat and stir in the yogurt, herbs, salt, and pepper. Mix thoroughly.

Preheat the oven to 300° F.

Cut 6 pieces of wax paper 10 by 6 inches. One at a time, place a chunk of lamb on a piece of the wax paper, spoon some of the yogurt mixture on top, and wrap the meat into a tight, square packet. Arrange the packets snugly in a baking pan. Bake for about 1 hour and 40 minutes, or until the paper is brown but not burned.

Serve immediately, with lamb still wrapped in paper. (Tearing into the brown packet is part of the fun, but the real reason is that the paper keeps the meat moist and tender.)

SERVES 6

HIRINI BRIZOLA KRASATI

(Pork Chops in Wine)

Although tavernas usually serve pork chops simply grilled, this dressier dish is also a taverna specialty. Often the waiter will flame the wine sauce at the table for a dramatic presentation. Sometimes cognac is used in this sauce, but that makes it too rich, I think. I prefer a good, dry red wine—what Greeks call Brousko.

<table>
<tr><td>6 large pork chops</td><td>2 tablespoons dried oregano</td></tr>
<tr><td>Salt and freshly ground black pepper to taste</td><td>⅓ cup pure olive oil</td></tr>
<tr><td></td><td>1½ cups dry red wine</td></tr>
</table>

Sprinkle the pork chops with salt and pepper and oregano. In a large skillet, heat the oil and sauté the pork chops over medium heat for about 7 to 10 minutes on each side, until golden brown. Add the wine, turn up the heat, and cook until most of the wine evaporates, 3 to 5 minutes. Serve immediately, spooning a little wine sauce on each chop.

SERVES 6

HIRINO ME PRASA

(Pork with Leeks in Egg-Lemon Sauce)

Thessalians serve this dish in winter, usually around Christmas, which is the traditional time for butchering the well-fed pigs. The lemony tang of this sauce adds the perfect balance to the rich taste of the pork.

¼ cup pure olive oil
3 pounds boneless lean leg of pork (fresh ham), cut into 6 large chunks
2 cups dry red wine
4 pounds leeks, white part only, thoroughly washed and cut into 1-inch pieces

Salt and freshly ground black pepper to taste
3 large eggs
Juice of 1 lemon

Heat the oil in a large pot. Add the pork and sauté until it turns light golden, about 5 minutes. Pour in the wine and stir to free any browned bits clinging to the pot. Add the leeks and season with salt and pepper. Simmer, partly covered, over medium-low heat for about 1½ hours. Stir frequently to prevent sticking, adding a little water as necessary to keep the meat moist. When the meat is tender and just a little liquid remains in the pot, remove from heat.

In a bowl, beat the eggs with the lemon juice until they are foamy. Pour the mixture over the hot meat and leeks, and shake the pot back and forth to distribute the sauce evenly. The heat of the pork and leeks will thicken the sauce slightly. Serve immediately.

NOTE: Reheat any leftovers over very low heat because the egg-lemon sauce will curdle if it is allowed to boil.

SERVES 6 TO 8

VARIATION: *Pork with Celery in Egg-Lemon Sauce*
Follow the master recipe, replacing the leeks with 3 bunches of celery, cut into 1-inch pieces, including leaves.

LAGOS SALMI

(Rabbit in Wine Sauce)

Autumn is hunting season in Greece, and hares are especially sought. Although most people in the countryside raise rabbits (and city people can buy them in the markets), hare has whiter meat and a milder taste. The dressed rabbit you can usually find in the poultry section of larger grocery stores will do fine, however.

⅓ cup pure olive oil
1 large onion, finely chopped
2 garlic cloves
1 rabbit (about 4 pounds), cut into small serving pieces
1½ cups dry white wine

4 tablespoons finely chopped fresh Italian parsley
1 teaspoon black peppercorns, or more to taste
Salt to taste
½ cup fresh orange juice

Heat the oil in a large pot. Add the onion, garlic, and rabbit pieces. Sauté over medium heat until the rabbit is golden brown on all sides and the onion is soft and golden, about 10 minutes. Pour the wine over the rabbit, stir gently, and turn the heat to high. Let the mixture bubble vigorously for a minute, then reduce heat to medium and simmer, uncovered, until half the wine has evaporated. Add the parsley, peppercorns, and salt and mix gently.

Add water barely to cover the rabbit and simmer, covered, over medium heat for about 50 minutes, or until the meat is tender. Stir in the orange juice and cook for 10 more minutes, until sauce has thickened slightly. Remove peppercorns with a slotted spoon if you prefer, or leave them in, as Greeks do. Serve hot, with pilaf on the side.

SERVES 6

LAGOS STIFATHO

(Rabbit Stew with Pearl Onions)

Stifatho is a type of stew that always features pearl onions in a tomato-based sauce. It can be made with beef or tongue but is especially delicious with rabbit.

⅓ cup pure olive oil
1 rabbit (about 4 pounds), cut
    into small serving pieces
    All-purpose flour for dredging
1½ cups dry red wine
2 tablespoons red wine vinegar
1 cup tomato sauce
3 bay leaves

4 garlic cloves
5 whole cloves
1 cinnamon stick
    Salt to taste
1 teaspoon black peppercorns, or
    more to taste
3 pounds pearl onions or very
    small white onions, peeled

Heat the oil in a large pot. Dredge each piece of rabbit in the flour, shake off any excess, and place the pieces, without crowding them, in the hot oil. Sauté the rabbit over medium heat until it is golden brown on all sides, about 10 minutes. Add the wine and vinegar, rocking the pot gently to distribute them evenly, and turn the heat to high. Let the liquid bubble vigorously for 5 to 10 minutes, until most of it has evaporated.

Add the tomato sauce and enough hot water just to cover the rabbit. Add the bay leaves, garlic, cloves, cinnamon stick, salt, and peppercorns and mix well. Cover and simmer over medium-low heat for about 45 minutes, or until half the liquid has evaporated.

Add the pearl onions, mixing them gently into the sauce, and replace the cover. Simmer for 30 minutes, or until onions are tender but still hold their shape. The sauce should be slightly thickened, just enough to coat a spoon. The traditional Greek way to serve this dish is with the whole herbs and spices left in, but you may strain them out if you prefer.

SERVES 6

Vegetables
(Lahanika)

At christening ceremonies in Greece, the priest anoints the forehead of the infant with olive oil. I used to think that this is why Greeks love olive oil so much: it's almost part of our religion.

Nowhere is this love of olive oil so evident as in vegetable dishes. Traditional recipes used to call for as much as two cups of olive oil in a dish to serve six persons. A vegetable dish was often the main course, served with lots of fresh bread to mop up the extra olive oil. This was especially true in the first two weeks of August, during which Greek Orthodox celebrate the Dormition of the Virgin Mary. It's a period of strict fasting—no meats allowed—and it also happens to be the time when summer vegetables are at their best.

In Karditsa, almost everyone could step into their garden to pick vegetables at the exact height of freshness. In summer, backyards were filled with tomato vines, zucchini plants, rows of green beans, and pepper plants. In winter, many people grew lettuce, green onions, and cabbages. Throughout the year, herb beds produced dill, parsley, mint, and a variety of other herbs.

My father was always too busy with his patients to care for a garden, as the other neighborhood men did. We usually bought our vegetables each Wednesday at the small outdoor farmers' market. In addition, my father's patients would bring their extra produce, as well as some of the wild arugula or dandelion greens that filled the fields around the town, which we used in fyllo pies or in cooked salads. When I first came to America I was amazed at how expensive arugula is, because I remembered it growing wild through the cracks in the village sidewalks!

Nowadays, the traditional ways of cooking vegetables are changing. As is true in America, Greeks are watching their weight and eating less fat. Though they still appreciate the flavor of good olive oil, they want less of it. I've adapted some of my favorite vegetable recipes from all over Greece to accommodate this trend toward lighter fare. I've substantially reduced the quantity of olive oil and the cooking time, but the Aegean flavor still comes through.

Some of these dishes make excellent light main courses, or you could serve them as accompaniments to grilled chicken, shish kebob, or any simple meat dish.

FASOLAKIA YAHNI

(Green Bean Stew)

If you use fresh, summer green beans and serve this dish with feta cheese on the side, it makes a lovely light supper. Of course, it also complements any roasted meat.

2 pounds fresh green beans, ends trimmed
3 large boiling potatoes, peeled and cut lengthwise in wedges
½ cup pure olive oil
2 large onions, coarsely chopped
2 garlic cloves, coarsely chopped

4 large ripe tomatoes, peeled, seeded, and chopped
4 tablespoons finely chopped Italian parsley
Salt and freshly ground black pepper to taste

Place the green beans in a large covered casserole and arrange the potatoes on top. Set aside.

Heat the olive oil in a large pot. Sauté the onions and garlic over medium heat for a few minutes, until lightly colored. Stir in the tomatoes and parsley, and sauté for a few more minutes, until sauce is well blended. Season with salt and pepper and pour over the beans and potatoes.

Cover the casserole and let the vegetables simmer over medium heat for about 30 minutes, until potatoes are tender and the sauce has thickened. Serve warm or cold.

SERVES 6

KOLOKITHIA YEMISTA ME RIZI

(Stuffed Zucchini with Rice)

My mother liked to serve the small, new zucchini of early summer in salads. For this recipe, which we had as a main course, along with feta cheese and crusty bread, she would wait until the end of June, when the zucchini were medium-size. (She'd never use the great big ones; she found them tough and flavorless.)

12 medium zucchini
¾ cup pure olive oil
3 large onions, finely chopped
1½ cups long-grain white rice
2 tablespoons finely chopped fresh dill
2 tablespoons finely chopped fresh Italian parsley

Salt and freshly ground black pepper to taste
¾ cup water
3 large eggs
Juice of 1 lemon

With a small teaspoon or melon baller, carefully scoop out the pulp of the zucchini, leaving a boat-shaped shell ½ inch thick. (This makes a much prettier presentation than simply slicing the zucchini in half lengthwise.) Finely chop the pulp and set it aside.

In a large skillet, heat the olive oil and sauté the onions over medium heat until they are soft and golden. Add the zucchini pulp, rice, dill, parsley, salt and pepper, and water. Mix well and simmer, covered, over medium heat for about 10 minutes, or until all the water has evaporated and the rice is half cooked.

With a small teaspoon, stuff the zucchini shells with the rice mixture. Arrange the shells in one layer in a very large covered skillet. (If they won't fit in one skillet, use two.) Add about 1 inch of water to the pan, cover tightly, and cook over medium-low heat for about 30 to 40 minutes, or until rice is cooked and zucchini are soft but not mushy. Remove from heat.

In a medium bowl, beat the eggs with the lemon juice until they are foamy. Spoon in some of the hot zucchini cooking liquid to warm the eggs and then pour the mixture over the zucchini. Tilt and rock the pan gently to distribute the egg-lemon sauce thoroughly. The heat of the zucchini will cook the sauce and thicken it slightly. (Do not let the sauce boil or it will curdle.) Serve hot or warm.

SERVES 6 AS A MAIN COURSE, 12 AS A SIDE DISH

BAMIES LATHERES *(Okra Stew)*

Okra, a favorite vegetable in Greece as well as in the American South, can be tricky to cook, since it will exude a gooey liquid if not handled correctly. As noted earlier, my mother's secret was to dip each pod before cooking in red wine vinegar. Also, she would rock the pan rather than stir the okra while cooking, as the pods are delicate and easy to mash.

2½ pounds fresh okra
1 cup red wine vinegar
½ cup pure olive oil
3 medium onions, finely chopped
2 garlic cloves, minced
3 large ripe tomatoes, peeled, seeded, and finely chopped
4 tablespoons finely chopped fresh Italian parsley
2 cups water
Salt and freshly ground black pepper to taste

Trim the okra stems and dip each pod for a few seconds into the vinegar. Set the okra aside.

Heat the oil in a large pot. Sauté the onions and garlic over medium heat until soft and lightly colored, about 5 minutes. Add the okra, tomatoes, parsley, and water, mixing gently by rocking the pan back and forth.

Cover and simmer over medium-low heat for about 30 to 40 minutes, or until the sauce has thickened and the okra is soft but not mushy. Season with salt and pepper. Serve warm or at room temperature.

SERVES 6

KOLOKYTHIA STO FOURNO ME TYRI

(Baked Zucchini with Cheese)

Kasseri cheese, which is one of two types specified for this recipe, is like a Greek mozzarella. It melts and browns nicely, while the feta adds tanginess.

½ cup oil, preferably corn or
    soybean oil, for frying
8 medium zucchini, cut
    lengthwise into thick slices
8 ounces feta cheese, crumbled
    (about 2 cups)

5 ounces kasseri cheese, shredded
    (a little more than 1 cup)
3 medium ripe tomatoes, thinly
    sliced
1 teaspoon dried oregano

Preheat the oven to 450° F.

In a large skillet, heat the oil and sauté the zucchini over medium-high heat until lightly colored and almost cooked, about 2 minutes. Place the zucchini on paper towels to absorb excess oil and then arrange the slices in layers in a medium rectangular baking pan. Spread the cheeses evenly over the zucchini, then cover with tomato slices. Sprinkle with the oregano and bake until the cheeses have melted, about 15 to 20 minutes. Serve immediately.

SERVES 6

AGINARES A LA POLITA

(Artichoke Hearts Polita Style)

This dish is popular among Greeks with Turkish roots (Greeks refer to Istanbul as Poli). It is a delectable dish to serve for a dinner party, well worth whatever trouble it takes to prepare the artichoke hearts for cooking. Serve with roasted lamb or veal.

6 large artichokes
3 large lemons
½ cup pure olive oil
2 large onions, thickly sliced
3 large carrots, peeled and thickly
  sliced
6 small potatoes, peeled and cut in
  half

5 tablespoons finely chopped fresh
  dill
Salt and freshly ground black
  pepper to taste
2 large eggs, beaten
1 tablespoon cornstarch

With a sharp knife, trim the stems of the artichokes, leaving about 1 inch below the globes. Pull off the hard dark green outer leaves, stopping at the tender light green inner ones. Peel the lower part of the globe and the stem, removing all the dark green remnants of the outer leaves and the tough skin of the stems. Gently pry open the remaining leaves, and with a small teaspoon or melon baller, carefully scrape out the chokes, leaving the hearts.

Halve one of the lemons and rub the halves over the artichoke hearts to prevent discoloration. Fill a large bowl with warm water and add the artichoke hearts and lemon halves. Soak for at least 30 minutes to remove any trace of bitterness in the artichokes.

Heat the oil in a large, shallow saucepan, and sauté the onions over medium heat until soft and golden, about 5 minutes. Add the artichoke hearts, then the carrots and potatoes. Sprinkle with dill and salt and pepper, and add water just to cover. Simmer over medium-low heat, tightly covered, for about 1 hour, or until vegetables are tender and most of the water has evaporated. Set aside.

In a medium bowl, combine the eggs, cornstarch, and juice of the remaining lemons. Add whatever hot liquid remains in the pan of vegetables; the sauce should be light yellow and thin. Pour the mixture into the saucepan, rocking to combine the sauce with the vegetables. Simmer briefly over low heat (do not allow to boil) until the sauce thickens slightly. Serve warm.

SERVES 6

MOUSAKAS LATHEROS *(Vegetarian Mousaka)*

I had the best version of this dish in a small taverna in Thessaloniki many years ago. Served in small pottery dishes, it looked like a soufflé.

When my mother prepared this dish, I loved to sneak some of the fried eggplant and put it on a large slice of crusty bread, topped with feta cheese. With a ripe tomato in the other hand, I had a very tasty summer snack.

4 medium eggplants
1 cup oil, preferably corn or
 soybean, for frying
3 medium potatoes, peeled and
 thinly sliced
2 large onions, thinly sliced
3 ripe large tomatoes, peeled,
 seeded, and finely chopped

3 garlic cloves, minced
 Salt and freshly ground black
  pepper to taste
1 cup milk
3 large eggs, lightly beaten
8 ounces feta cheese, crumbled
 (about 2 cups)

Preheat the oven to 350° F.

Remove the stems from eggplants and cut lengthwise into thin slices. Sprinkle lightly with salt and set aside to drain in a colander.

Heat the oil in a large skillet. Lightly sauté the potato slices over medium heat until they start turning golden, about 2 minutes. Remove from the oil with a slotted spoon and set aside. In the same pan, sauté the onions until they are soft and golden, then remove from the oil and set aside. Add the eggplant to the skillet and sauté until soft and lightly colored. Remove from the skillet and layer the vegetables in a medium baking pan, beginning with the eggplant, then the potatoes, then the onions, until all of the ingredients are used.

In a bowl, combine the tomatoes, garlic, and salt and pepper, and spread the mixture over the vegetables. In another bowl, thoroughly mix the milk, eggs, and feta cheese. Pour this over the tomatoes. Rock the baking dish gently to distribute the cheese mixture evenly. Bake for 45 minutes, until the top is golden brown and crusty. Serve warm.

SERVES 6

IMAM BAYILDI *(Imam's Special)*

Another recipe brought over by Greeks from Asia Minor, this stuffed eggplant would make a lovely lunch or light supper served with plenty of crusty bread. Don't be afraid of the large quantity of salt in this recipe. It is used to remove excess moisture and bitterness from the eggplants and will not remain in the finished dish.

3 medium eggplants
⅓ cup salt
1¾ cups pure olive oil
3 medium onions, thinly sliced
3 ripe large tomatoes, peeled, seeded, and coarsely chopped
3 garlic cloves, minced
6 tablespoons finely chopped fresh Italian parsley

Salt and freshly ground black pepper to taste
Pinch of sugar
8 ounces feta cheese, crumbled (about 2 cups)
2 cups tomato juice

Wash the eggplants, trim the stems, and cut in half lengthwise. Fill a large pot with warm water and dissolve the salt in it. Add the eggplants and soak for about 1 hour. The water will turn brownish. Drain thoroughly.

Preheat the oven to 400° F.

Heat 1½ cups of the olive oil in a large skillet. Fry the eggplants over medium heat for about 5 minutes, until brown and limp. Drain on paper towels and arrange in a baking dish.

In a medium saucepan, combine the remaining ¼ cup olive oil, onions, tomatoes, garlic, parsley, salt and pepper, and sugar. Simmer over medium heat, uncovered, for 15 minutes, or until sauce has thickened.

Using a teaspoon or melon baller, scoop out some of the eggplant pulp to make a shallow shell. Spoon the tomato mixture into each eggplant half and sprinkle with the feta cheese. Pour the tomato juice over the eggplants and bake for about 30 minutes, until the cheese turns light brown. Rock the pan to swirl the sauce all around.

Serve hot or warm, with crusty bread to mop up all the sauce.

SERVES 6

DOMATOPIPERIES YEMISTES

(Stuffed Tomatoes and Peppers)

My aunt Vita, a very particular shopper, knew how to choose the best tomatoes and peppers, which is the secret of this dish. The tomatoes have to be large and ripe, but firm; the peppers thin-skinned and fresh, and shaped so they will stand straight up on their bottoms.

Aunt Vita's other secrets were to sprinkle the insides of the scooped-out tomatoes with a bit of sugar to enhance their summery sweetness, and to stuff the vegetables loosely so that when the rice expands, it won't rupture the skins.

6 large, ripe, firm tomatoes
6 large sweet green peppers
1 tablespoon sugar
1 cup pure olive oil
3 large onions, finely chopped
5 tablespoons finely chopped
    Italian parsley

5 tablespoons finely chopped fresh
    dill
3 cups long-grain white rice
2 cups tomato juice
    Salt and freshly ground black
      pepper to taste

Wipe tomatoes and peppers with a damp paper towel. With a small, sharp knife, neatly slice off and set aside their stem ends for use later as covers.

With a small spoon, scrape out the seeds and ribs from the peppers and discard. Scoop out the pulp from the tomatoes and reserve. Arrange the tomato and pepper shells in a baking pan. Sprinkle the inside of the tomatoes with the sugar.

Heat ½ cup of oil in a large skillet. Sauté the onions over medium heat until soft and golden, about 5 minutes. Stir in the reserved tomato pulp, parsley, dill, and rice; simmer, partly covered, over low heat for about 10 minutes. If the mixture gets dry while simmering, add a little water. The rice should still be firm at this point.

Preheat the oven to 400° F.

Stuff the tomatoes and peppers no more than three-quarters full with the rice mixture. Place the reserved tomato and pepper lids on the vegetables.

Pour the tomato juice and the remaining oil over the vegetables. Sprinkle with salt and pepper and bake for about 30 to 40 minutes, until the rice is done and the vegetables color lightly. Serve warm or cold.

SERVES 6

BRIAMI *(Vegetable Stew)*

A little like a Greek ratatouille, this summery combination is good hot or cold, as a side dish with roasted or grilled meats, or served with bread and cheese as a luncheon dish.

2 pounds medium potatoes,
    peeled and cut into quarters
1 pound medium zucchini, thickly
    sliced
2 medium eggplants, unpeeled,
    cut into large chunks
3 large onions, thickly sliced
3 medium sweet green peppers,
    seeded, ribbed, and thickly
    sliced

1 bunch fresh Italian parsley,
    finely chopped
4 large ripe tomatoes, peeled,
    seeded, and coarsely chopped
    Salt and freshly ground black
    pepper to taste
½ cup pure olive oil

Preheat the oven to 400° F.

In a large baking pan, combine the potatoes, zucchini, eggplants, onions, green peppers, and parsley. Spread the tomatoes over this mixture and season with the salt and pepper. Pour in the olive oil and add enough warm water to bring the liquid to half the depth of the vegetables. Bake uncovered for about 1 hour, or until vegetables are tender and sauce has thickened. Serve warm or cold.

SERVES 6

Arakas me Kremythakia

(Green Peas with Green Onions)

When I was little, it was my job to shell the peas for this dish. I loved their sweet, crunchy taste so much that if my mother didn't watch me carefully, I'd eat most of them straight from the shell before she could cook them.

If you grow your own peas, or can get them in the spring when they are fresh and small, you can cook them in their pods. (Sugar snaps are also good cooked in this manner.) Larger peas should be shelled.

½ cup pure olive oil
10 green onions, green and white parts finely chopped
2 pounds fresh green peas in the shell

3 tablespoons finely chopped fresh dill
Salt and freshly ground black pepper to taste
¾ cup warm water

In a large saucepan, heat the oil and sauté the green onions over medium heat until soft and golden, about 5 minutes. Add the peas, dill, salt and pepper, and water. Simmer over medium-low heat, partly covered, for about 20 minutes, or until peas are cooked and a little thin sauce is left in the pan. Serve warm or cold.

SERVES 6

Lahanorizo *(Cabbage and Rice Stew)*

Another popular dish during fasting times, Lahanorizo can be a meal in itself when sprinkled with lots of grated kefalotiri cheese. This is one of many Aegean dishes always served with plenty of lemon wedges. Greeks use fresh lemon juice to season their food the way many other people use salt.

4 tablespoons (½ stick) unsalted butter
1 medium onion, finely chopped

1 medium head green cabbage, coarsely shredded
1½ cups tomato sauce

1 cup water
1½ cups long-grain white rice
Salt and freshly ground black
pepper to taste

Grated kefalotiri cheese
(optional)

Lemon wedges for garnish

Melt the butter in a large pot and lightly sauté the onion over medium heat until it is soft and golden, about 3 minutes. Add the cabbage and continue to sauté for 5 minutes, stirring constantly. Stir in the tomato sauce, water, and rice. Cover and cook over medium-low heat until the rice is cooked and there is only a little liquid left in the bottom of the pan, about 20 minutes. Season with salt and pepper. Sprinkle with grated cheese, if desired. Serve hot, garnished with lemon wedges.

SERVES 6

SPANOKORIZO *(Spinach and Rice Casserole)*

I like to serve this as a side dish with roasted chicken or other plain meats, although it also makes a wonderful winter lunch.

½ cup pure olive oil
6 green onions, green and white
  parts finely chopped
3 pounds fresh spinach, washed,
  trimmed, and coarsely
  chopped
1½ cups long-grain white rice

3 tablespoons finely chopped
  fresh dill
2 cups water
  Salt and freshly ground black
  pepper to taste

Lemon wedges for garnish

Heat the oil in a large pot. Sauté the green onions over medium heat until soft and golden, about 3 minutes. Stir in the spinach and sauté until wilted, about 3 minutes. Add the rice, dill, and water, and stir. Cover and simmer over medium-low heat until the rice is cooked and all the liquid is absorbed, about 15 to 20 minutes. Season with salt and pepper. Serve warm, garnished with lots of lemon wedges.

SERVES 6

PATATES ME TYRIA

(Potatoes with Cheese)

My mother insisted that the combination of kefalotiri, feta, and kasseri cheeses was the only proper one for this dish. I agree that feta is a must for its spicy and salty taste, but I generally combine it with anything else available in my refrigerator: Swiss, cheddar, mozzarella, or any other cheese that melts easily. You can bake this in one large pan, or in individual pottery dishes for a dressier presentation. This was always a main course for my family, but in smaller portions it makes a lovely first course for a winter dinner.

3 tablespoons unsalted butter, melted

2 pounds medium potatoes, peeled and thinly sliced
Freshly ground black pepper

4 ounces kefalotiri cheese, grated (about 1 cup)

8 ounces feta cheese, crumbled (about 2 cups)

6 ounces kasseri cheese, shredded (about 1½ cups)

Preheat the oven to 350° F.

With a pastry brush, generously butter a medium baking pan, using some of the melted butter. Cover the bottom of the pan with a layer of sliced potatoes and sprinkle with pepper. Spread about one-third of the cheeses over the top. Add another layer of potatoes, pepper, and cheese, continuing in this manner until all the ingredients are used and ending with the cheese. Bake for about 1 hour, or until top is puffy and golden. Serve immediately.

SERVES 6

PRASA YAHNI

(Stewed Leeks)

In the winter we would put on our mud boots to walk through the rain to the central market of Karditsa, where we selected vegetables from among the wet baskets of cabbages, cauliflowers, leeks, spinach, broccoli, potatoes, beets, lettuce, celery, and onions. Yahni, which means stew, is a popular way of cooking winter vegetables in Greece. We would usually add jars of garden tomatoes preserved from the summer before, but ordinary canned tomatoes can also be used.

2½ pounds leeks, well washed, white parts cut into ¾-inch pieces
2 cups water
2 large celery stalks, leaves included, finely chopped
4 large carrots, peeled and thinly sliced
1 large onion, finely chopped

4 large ripe tomatoes, peeled, seeded, and finely chopped
3 bay leaves
½ cup pure olive oil
3 tablespoons red wine vinegar
Pinch of ground cinnamon
Salt and freshly ground black pepper to taste

Put the leeks and ½ cup of the water into a large pot. Simmer over low heat, covered, until the leeks begin to wilt. Add the celery, carrots, onion, tomatoes, bay leaves, olive oil, vinegar, and cinnamon. Stir in remaining water.

Cover the pot and cook over medium-low heat until the liquid is reduced to a thick sauce, about 30 to 40 minutes. Season with salt and pepper. Remove the bay leaves if you prefer, although Greek cooks always leave them in. Serve hot or warm.

SERVES 6

Fyllo Pies
(Pites)

When my aunt Harikleia baked a pita, the whole neighborhood knew. First thing in the morning, everyone could smell the charcoal burning as Harikleia prepared the gastra—a huge, shallow iron pan that is used, especially in our area of Thessalia, as an outside oven—in her backyard. Harikleia would fill the pan with charcoal and let the coals slowly turn ashy. When the coals were just right, she would place on top of them a baking dish filled with her pita, and cover the pan with its heavy iron lid. Being an expert in pites, Harikleia would bake them only in the gastra. A pita baked in a gastra and one baked in a conventional oven are as different in taste as a charbroiled steak is from a pan-fried one.

I don't make my pites in a gastra now, but I do still use Harikleia's secrets for working with the dough and fillings. Some of my earliest memories are of watching her make fyllo pastry. When I was five or six, she would let me help. She would first knead the dough with her strong, sturdy hands that were as white as the flour she was using. And then she would give me a small piece of the kneaded dough, saying, "That's your share. Make your own pita." She would finish rolling out her smooth, thin fyllo sheets, and I would still be struggling in vain to give my dough some shape.

"Stop torturing the dough!" she would say. "Let me help you." And with her two loving hands guiding mine, very soon my own fyllo sheets were formed on the table.

The last time I saw Harikleia was in the summer of 1983, when I went back to Greece for a month's vacation. I spent a few days with my parents and other relatives up in Kastania, my father's birthplace, and of course, Harikleia prepared some of my favorite pites for me. Although she looked frail, she worked on the sheets with the same certainty as always. She asked me if in America women liked to make pites with homemade fyllo dough.

"I don't think so," I answered. "They would think it's too much work."

She looked surprised. "If a Greek woman can do it, why not an American? What's wrong with their hands? Are they sick?"

Harikleia spent much of the following year in the hospital. No one needed to inform me of her death. The night before she died I saw her in a dream, preparing Spanokopita (Spinach Pie, page 132). In our area, Spanokopita is one of the dishes we always prepare for sad occasions. I knew it was a bad dream.

This chapter is dedicated to her. Except for some interesting specialties that I tasted in other parts of Greece, all of the following recipes are from Harikleia. Although I receive compliments frequently on my pites, I never feel that they quite measure up to the ones of my childhood. Maybe it's the gastra that I miss—but more likely it's the loving hands of Harikleia.

A pita is any type of pie where the filling is enclosed top and bottom in fyllo pastry. (Don't confuse a Greek pita, which means simply "pie," with the Middle Eastern pita bread, something not widely used in Greece.) The filling can be between two layers of fyllo, as in conventional pies, or it can be wrapped or rolled up in the fyllo and formed into various shapes. We usually eat pites as a main course, but they make excellent first courses as well.

In Greece, the pastry is usually either made at home, rolled out in thin, elastic sheets, or bought fresh at special shops. It is also available frozen in supermarkets, though the commercial sheets are much thinner than the homemade. Following is a recipe for basic fyllo dough.

Fyllo

You must use homemade fyllo right away, as it does not keep well.

1 pound all-purpose flour
1 teaspoon salt
1 cup water

1 teaspoon red wine vinegar
½ cup pure olive oil

Sift flour and salt into a bowl. Stir in water and vinegar. Add olive oil slowly, mixing it with your hands until smooth. Knead well, stretching the dough until it is soft and elastic. You may need to add some water to achieve the proper consistency. Cover with a towel and set in a cool place for 1 hour. Divide dough into quarters and roll each piece out into a thin, elastic sheet.

MAKES 4 FYLLO SHEETS, OR ABOUT 1 POUND

NOTE: You can also buy frozen sheets of fyllo at many large supermarkets. I recommend, however, that you look for a Greek or Middle Eastern specialty store in your area because their stock of frozen fyllo turns over faster and is therefore fresher. Almost all the recipes that follow call for commercial fyllo, but if you wish to use your homemade dough, remember that one sheet of homemade replaces four sheets of commercial fyllo.

Store any frozen fyllo that you are not planning to use immediately in the freezer. The day before using it, thaw the package in the refrigerator and bring it to room temperature for about one hour before opening.

Once you open the package, it's important to work fast, because commercial fyllo sheets are so thin that they dry out easily. Don't worry, though, if some of the sheets tear or crumble. Just put another sheet on top and nobody will notice. If you are interrupted in your work for any length of time, be sure to cover the dough with a damp towel until you can get back to it.

Basic fyllo can be used in almost any of the *pita* recipes. For some recipes, however, a more substantial dough is better. Fillings that are particularly rich or moist, such as those for *Kolokythopita* (Zucchini Pie, page 136) and *Koto-pita* (Chicken Pie, page 137), would turn the thin fyllo leaves to mush. For these, Greeks usually use puff pastry, which we buy ready-made.

Many of the *pita* recipes call for clarified butter, directions on page 71.

AGINAROPITA *(Artichoke Pie)*

My aunt made this dish as her specialty. The sharp and salty cheeses add flavor to the rather bland artichokes. You can substitute good-quality Parmesan for the kefalotiri, if you like.

¼ cup pure olive oil

6 green onions, green and white parts finely chopped

6 large artichoke hearts, uncooked, cut into large pieces

5 tablespoons finely chopped fresh dill

3 large eggs, beaten

8 ounces feta cheese, crumbled (about 2 cups)

½ cup milk

½ cup grated kefalotiri cheese

Freshly ground black pepper to taste

Unsalted clarified butter (page 71), to grease pan

1 pound *sfoliata* (puff pastry)

1 egg yolk, beaten

Heat the oil in a large saucepan. Add the green onions and sauté over medium heat until they are soft and golden, about 5 minutes. Add the artichoke hearts, cover with warm water, and cook over medium heat, partly covered, for about 1 hour, or until almost all of the water has evaporated and the artichoke hearts are tender. Remove from the heat and let cool.

Put the artichoke mixture in a large bowl and add the dill, eggs, feta cheese, milk, and kefalotiri cheese, stirring well to blend. Season with pepper.

Preheat the oven to 350° F.

Grease a 9 by 13-inch baking pan with some clarified butter. Divide the puff pastry in half. Roll out one half into a sheet slightly larger than the baking pan and about ¼ inch thick. Place this in the bottom and up the sides of the baking pan. Pour in the artichoke filling, spreading it to all corners. Roll out the other piece of pastry about the same size as the pan and place it on top of the filling. Seal the edges by pressing lightly with your fingers or a fork. Brush the top with the beaten egg yolk. Bake for about 45 minutes, until light brown. Serve hot.

SERVES 6 TO 8

SPANOKOPITA *(Spinach Pie)*

This may be the most well known of all the Greek pites. You can taste Spanokopita in homes all over Greece and at many tavernas; it will never taste the same twice. In some areas, for instance, the spinach is mixed with leeks. In Thessalia we usually mix the spinach with rathikia, *a kind of chicory, and other wild greens that abound in the area. Many people don't use feta cheese, especially during Lent. Others use butter instead of olive oil.*

In the following recipe I use only spinach, but feel free to replace part of it with any other kind of greens. I always use olive oil instead of butter for this pie because I feel its flavor enhances that of the greens and also, of course, because it's healthier!

3 pounds fresh spinach
1 tablespoon salt
¾ cup pure olive oil
10 green onions, green and white
    parts finely chopped
4 tablespoons finely chopped
    fresh dill

Salt and freshly ground black
    pepper to taste
3 large eggs, lightly beaten
8 ounces feta cheese
1 pound fyllo pastry

Preheat the oven to 350° F.

Wash the spinach thoroughly and drain. Chop it coarsely and put it into a large colander. Sprinkle it with about 1 tablespoon of salt and let it sit for at least 30 minutes. Then, a handful of spinach at a time, squeeze out all the excess water and salt. (This technique removes any bitterness and does not leave the spinach salty. Some cooks, however, prefer to blanch the spinach in boiling water until wilted and then squeeze dry.)

In a large skillet, heat ¼ cup of the olive oil and sauté the green onions until translucent, about 5 minutes. Remove from the heat and add spinach, dill, salt and pepper, eggs, and feta cheese, stirring until well combined.

With a pastry brush, coat a 9 by 13-inch baking pan with some of the remaining oil. Lay a sheet of fyllo dough in the pan, brushing it with olive oil. Layer 4 more sheets of fyllo in the pan, brushing each with oil. Spread half the spinach mixture over the fyllo. Cover this with 3 more sheets of fyllo, brushing oil on each sheet. Spread the rest of the spinach mixture over this and layer 5 more sheets of fyllo on top, again brushing each, including the top sheet, with oil.

With a sharp knife, score the *Spanokopita* into serving squares before baking. Bake for about 40 minutes, or until golden and crisp. Serve warm or cold.

SERVES 6 TO 8

FASOLAKIA PITA *(Green Bean Pie)*

Try this as a side dish with roasted or grilled meats, or as a first course to a simple summer meal.

4 tablespoons (½ stick) unsalted
   butter
3 medium onions, thinly sliced
2 garlic cloves, finely minced
½ pound fresh green beans, ends
   trimmed and julienned
3 tablespoons finely chopped fresh
   Italian parsley

Salt and freshly ground black
   pepper to taste
½ cup (1 stick) unsalted butter,
   melted and clarified (page 71)
1 pound fyllo pastry

Preheat the oven to 350° F.

Melt the butter in a medium pot. Add the onions and garlic and sauté until they turn soft and golden, about 5 minutes. Add the green beans and cook over low heat, covered, for about 15 minutes or until almost tender, stirring occasionally. Stir in parsley and season with salt and pepper.

With a pastry brush, coat the bottom of a 9 by 13-inch baking pan with some of the clarified butter and line it with a sheet of fyllo dough. Brush the fyllo dough with some more of the butter. In this manner, layer 5 more sheets of fyllo dough in the pan, brushing each lightly with the butter. Spread the green beans evenly over the fyllo and cover with 6 more sheets of fyllo dough, brushing each lightly with butter. With a sharp knife, score the top in serving squares. Bake for about 35 minutes, or until golden and crisp. Serve warm.

SERVES 6 TO 8

MELITZANOPITA

(Eggplant Pie)

This is a light summer specialty, when eggplants are at their peak. Be sure to choose only ripe, perfect eggplants—otherwise they can be bitter.

¼ cup pure olive oil
2 medium onions, finely chopped
2 large eggplants, unpeeled, coarsely chopped
Salt and freshly ground black pepper to taste
Pinch of ground cinnamon

⅓ cup water
8 ounces feta cheese, crumbled (about 2 cups)
3 large eggs, lightly beaten
¾ cup (1½ sticks) unsalted butter, melted and clarified (page 71)
1 pound fyllo pastry

Preheat the oven to 350° F.

Heat the oil in a medium saucepan. Add the onions and sauté lightly over medium heat until they are soft and golden, about 5 minutes. Add the eggplant and sauté until soft, about 5 to 10 minutes more. Season with salt, pepper, and cinnamon. Add water to the pan, mix, and simmer over low heat until all of the water has evaporated, about 15 minutes. Add the feta cheese and eggs, and stir until smooth.

With a pastry brush, grease a 9 by 13-inch baking pan with some of the clarified butter. Line the bottom of the pan with a sheet of fyllo dough, brushing it lightly with clarified butter. In this manner, layer 4 more sheets of fyllo pastry in the bottom of the pan, brushing each with the butter. Spread half the eggplant mixture over the fyllo and cover with 3 sheets of fyllo pastry, brushing each with butter. Spread with the remaining eggplant mixture and cover with 5 more sheets of fyllo, brushing each with butter. Butter the top sheet generously. With a sharp knife, score the pie into serving squares. Sprinkle lightly with a little water.

Bake for about 40 minutes, or until golden and crisp. Serve hot or warm.

SERVES 6 TO 8

PASTITSIO ME ARAKA

(Pasta Pie with Green Peas)

My mother always enclosed her Pastitsio *with fyllo dough because she thought it looked more finished and attractive. I find that the flaky fyllo dough provides a nice contrast to the soft pasta beneath.*

1 pound large elbow pasta
4 tablespoons unsalted butter
4 cups green peas, cooked
1 pound feta cheese, crumbled
  (about 4 cups)
  Freshly ground black pepper to
  taste

6 tablespoons (¾ stick) unsalted
  butter, melted and clarified
  (page 71)
½ pound fyllo pastry

Preheat the oven to 350° F.

Cook the pasta in a large pot of boiling, salted water just until done. (Greeks like their pasta a little softer than al dente.) Drain and set aside.

Melt the butter in a large skillet over medium heat. Add the peas and sauté for a few minutes, just until hot.

In a large bowl, combine the pasta, peas and butter, feta cheese, and pepper and mix well.

With a pastry brush, grease a 9 by 13-inch baking pan with some clarified butter. Line the bottom and sides with a sheet of fyllo dough, brushing it with a little of the clarified butter. In this manner, layer 3 more fyllo sheets, brushing each with butter. Spread the pasta mixture on top of the fyllo. Cover with 4 more fyllo sheets, brushing each with butter. Brush the top sheet generously. Bake until the top is golden and crisp, about 45 minutes. Serve hot or warm.

SERVES 6 TO 8

KOLOKYTHOPITA *(Zucchini Pie)*

If you grow zucchini yourself, or your neighbor likes to bestow some of the bounty on you, you'll never again need to wonder what to do with the big zucchini that are so plentiful at the end of summer. Just grate them and make this delicious pie. Please note that the recipe uses a different type of dough because commercial fyllo would become too soggy from all the moisture in the zucchini, along with the eggs and milk.

4 cups all-purpose flour	Pinch of salt
1 egg yolk	1 cup warm water
1 tablespoon olive oil	

FILLING

6 to 8 large zucchini, coarsely shredded	5 large eggs, lightly beaten
1 teaspoon salt	1½ cups milk
10 ounces feta cheese, crumbled (a little less than 3 cups)	¾ cup (1½ sticks) unsalted butter, melted

To make the dough, combine the flour, egg yolk, oil, and salt in a large bowl. Slowly add warm water, mixing thoroughly until the dough is smooth and soft. Cover with a tea towel and let stand in a warm place for at least 1 hour.

To make the filling, put the shredded zucchini in a large colander. Sprinkle with the salt and let stand for about 1 hour. Taking a handful of zucchini at a time, squeeze out as much water as possible and place drained zucchini in a large bowl. Add the cheese, eggs, and milk and mix well.

Preheat the oven to 350° F.

Knead the dough for a few minutes and divide it into thirds. Roll out each third into a sheet about ⅛ inch thick and big enough to generously cover the bottom of a 9 by 13-inch baking pan.

With a pastry brush, coat the pan with a little melted butter. Place 1 sheet of dough in the bottom of the pan and brush it lightly with melted butter. Spread half of the zucchini mixture over the pastry. Cover with the second sheet of pastry and brush lightly with melted butter. Cover with the remaining zucchini and then with the last sheet of pastry, buttering it generously.

Bake for about 40 to 50 minutes, or until the crust colors lightly. Increase the oven temperature to 450° F. and bake for a few minutes more, until the top is golden brown and crusty. Serve hot or warm.

SERVES 6 TO 8

KOTOPITA *(Chicken Pie)*

Binding together the chicken and onions in this pita *is lots of melted cheese. Puff pastry is the best choice here, because it holds up to the rich and creamy filling.*

4 tablespoons (½ stick) unsalted butter

4 medium onions, thinly sliced

1 medium chicken (about 3 pounds), boiled, skin and bones discarded, and meat coarsely chopped

12 ounces feta cheese, cut into small cubes (about 3 cups)

12 ounces kefalotiri or Parmesan cheese, coarsely shredded (about 3 cups)

3 tablespoons finely chopped fresh Italian parsley

Ground nutmeg to taste

Salt and freshly ground black pepper to taste

1½ pounds *sfoliata* (puff pastry)

Preheat the oven to 350° F.

Melt the butter in a large saucepan. Add the onions and sauté over medium heat until they are soft and golden, about 5 minutes. Combine well with the chicken, cheeses, parsley, and nutmeg. Season with salt and pepper.

Using a small pastry brush, grease a 9 by 13-inch baking pan with a little more melted butter. Divide the pastry into 2 sheets. Roll out one sheet slightly larger than the pan. Place it in the bottom and up the sides of the pan. Spread the chicken filling over the pastry. Roll out the second sheet just big enough to cover the top and place it over the chicken filling. Seal the edges by pressing lightly with your fingers or a fork. Bake for about 40 minutes, until the pastry is puffy and light brown. Serve hot or warm.

SERVES 6 TO 8

KOTORIZOPITA *(Chicken Rice Pie)*

I encountered this pita in Epirus, a mountainous region near Thessalia. Here, as in my home, everyone raises a few chickens in the backyard and, of course, looks for interesting chicken dishes like this pita.

1 small chicken (about 2 pounds)
2 large onions, cut in half
3 cups long-grain white rice
4 tablespoons (½ stick) unsalted butter
Salt and freshly ground black pepper to taste

3 large eggs, lightly beaten
½ cup (1 stick) unsalted butter, melted and clarified (page 71)
½ pound fyllo pastry

Preheat the oven to 350° F.

Wash the chicken and place it and the onions in a large pot. Cover with water and bring to a boil over high heat. Reduce heat and simmer, partly covered, until chicken is cooked, about 45 minutes. Remove chicken and onions from the pot and set aside. Measure out 6 cups of broth. (Add water if there is not enough.) Put the broth in a pot and bring to a boil. Add the rice, reduce heat, and simmer, partly covered, until all the liquid evaporates and rice is cooked, about 20 minutes.

Discard the skin and bones of the chicken. Cut chicken and onions into small pieces. Melt the 4 tablespoons of butter in a large skillet over medium heat. Add onions and chicken and sauté for 5 minutes. Remove from heat, mix in the rice, and season with salt and pepper. Add eggs and mix until smooth.

With a pastry brush, coat a 9 by 13-inch baking pan with some of the clarified butter. Lay one sheet of fyllo dough in the bottom of the pan and brush it lightly with clarified butter. In this manner, layer 4 more sheets of pastry in the bottom of the pan, brushing each lightly with clarified butter. Spread the chicken mixture over the pastry and cover with 4 more sheets of fyllo dough, brushing each lightly with clarified butter. Brush the top with more butter and score into serving pieces with a sharp knife. Bake for about 45 minutes, until golden and crisp. Serve hot or warm.

SERVES 6 TO 8

KREATOPITA ME MOSHARI KAI ARNI
(Meat Pie with Beef and Lamb)

Kreatopites, or meat pies, are the kind of pites Greeks always eat for joyful events. We prepare them for the first Sunday of the Carnival before Lent; we also serve them for weddings and birthday parties. In some areas a Kreatopita is the traditional New Year's Day meal. This one is a specialty from my region, Thessalia.

2 tablespoons (¼ stick) unsalted butter
2 large onions, finely chopped
1 pound lean ground beef
1 pound ground lamb
1 cup dry white wine
    Salt and freshly ground black pepper to taste
Pinch of ground cinnamon
4 tablespoons finely chopped fresh Italian parsley
½ cup pine nuts
4 hard-boiled eggs, coarsely diced
¾ cup (1½ sticks) unsalted butter, melted and clarified (page 71)
1 pound fyllo pastry

Preheat the oven to 350° F.

Melt the butter in a large saucepan. Add the onions and meat and sauté over medium heat until the onions are soft and golden and the meat turns brown, about 10 minutes. Add the wine and stir until the liquid evaporates. Season with salt, pepper, and cinnamon. Gently stir in the parsley, pine nuts, and eggs. Set aside.

With a pastry brush, grease a 9 by 13-inch baking pan with a little of the clarified butter. Place a sheet of fyllo dough in the pan, and brush it with clarified butter. In this manner, layer 5 sheets of fyllo dough.

Spread half of the meat filling over the fyllo dough. Cover this with 4 sheets of fyllo dough, brushing each with clarified butter. Spread the remaining meat filling on top. Cover with 5 sheets of fyllo dough, brushing each with butter. Butter the top generously and score the pie into serving squares with a sharp knife.

Bake for about 1 hour, or until golden and crisp. Serve hot.

SERVES 6 TO 8

PITA ME THALASSINA *(Seafood Pie)*

Like all Greek food, pites *reflect the regions they are from; and an Aegean* pita, *such as this one, is certainly going to have seafood in it. You can use sole, cod, or any other firm, white fish with few bones.*

7 tablespoons unsalted butter
5 tablespoons all-purpose flour
1 tablespoon Dijon mustard
    Salt and red pepper to taste
2 cups milk
12 ounces kefalotiri or Parmesan
    cheese, finely shredded (about
    3 cups)
1 medium onion, finely chopped
8 ounces lump crab meat, picked
    over and coarsely chopped

8 ounces small shrimp, cooked
    and peeled
8 ounces white fish fillet, cooked
    and cut into chunks
4 tablespoons finely chopped
    fresh Italian parsley
¾ cup (1½ sticks) unsalted butter,
    melted and clarified (page 71)
1 pound fyllo pastry

Preheat the oven to 350° F.

Melt 4 tablespoons of the butter in a medium saucepan. Whisk in the flour, mustard, salt, and red pepper, stirring until smooth. Add the milk, whisking over medium heat until the mixture thickens, about 10 to 15 minutes. Remove from heat and add the cheese, stirring until it melts. Set aside.

Melt the remaining 3 tablespoons of butter in a large skillet. Add the onion and sauté over medium heat until soft and golden, about 5 minutes. Add the crab, shrimp, fish, parsley, and the cheese mixture and stir over medium heat for a few minutes, until uniformly blended.

With a pastry brush, coat a 9 by 13-inch baking pan with some of the clarified butter. Line the bottom with a sheet of fyllo dough and brush it with clarified butter. In this manner, layer 4 more sheets of fyllo dough in the bottom of the pan, brushing each with butter.

Spread half the seafood mixture on the fyllo sheets and cover with 3 fyllo sheets, brushing each with clarified butter. Spread with the remaining seafood mixture. Cover with 5 more fyllo sheets, brushing each with clarified butter. Brush the top sheet generously.

With a sharp knife, score the pie into serving squares. Bake for 40 to 50 minutes, until golden and crisp. Serve immediately.

SERVES 6 TO 8

GARITHOPITA *(Shrimp Pie)*

I first tasted these flaky pies in a small taverna on the island of Corfu. The puff pastry folds up over the shrimp filling to make charming, individual pockets.

½ pound *sfoliata* (puff pastry)
6 ounces kasseri cheese, shredded (about 1½ cups)
2 large ripe tomatoes, peeled, seeded, and finely chopped
1 large sweet green pepper, seeds and ribs removed, finely chopped

12 large shrimp, peeled, deveined, and cut in half crosswise
Dried oregano to taste
Salt and freshly ground black pepper to taste

Preheat the oven to 400° F.

Roll out the pastry into a 16 by 16-inch square, ¼ inch thick. Cut it into six 4 by 8-inch pieces. Place equal amounts of cheese, tomatoes, and pepper and 4 pieces of shrimp on each square. Sprinkle each with oregano, salt, and pepper. Fold the pastry over to make 4-inch pouches and pinch the edges together. Make sure no filling is leaking out.

Arrange the pouches on a buttered baking sheet and bake for about 30 minutes, or until they are light brown and puffy. Serve hot or warm.

SERVES 6

KADAIFI TYROPITA

(Shredded Dough Cheese Pie)

Shredded kadaifi *dough, which can be made only with a special machine, can be found ready-made in Middle Eastern markets or in some well-stocked grocery stores. It is traditionally used to make desserts, but I recently started using it instead of regular fyllo to make a special kind of* tyropita. *This makes a festive presentation, a little like a soufflé. Serve it in very small portions, as it is very rich.*

½ cup (1 stick) unsalted butter,
    melted and clarified (page 71)
1 pound *kadaifi* dough
8 ounces feta cheese, crumbled
    (about 2 cups)
8 ounces kasseri cheese,
    shredded (about 2 cups)

¾ cup heavy cream
1½ cups milk
4 large eggs
  Freshly ground black pepper to
    taste

With a pastry brush, generously coat the sides and bottom of a 9 by 13-inch baking pan with some of the butter.

Pull the compacted shreds of dough apart. Cover the bottom of the pan with half the dough. Drizzle half of the butter over the dough, then sprinkle with the feta and kasseri cheeses. Cover the cheeses completely with the remaining *kadaifi*. Drizzle with the remaining butter.

In a medium bowl, beat together the cream, milk, eggs, and pepper until smooth. Pour evenly over the pie. Set aside for 1 hour.

Preheat the oven to 350° F.

Bake the pie for 1 hour, or until top is golden and firm to the touch. Serve hot.

SERVES 12 TO 16

GALATOPITA *(Milk Pie)*

This traditional Thessalian pie will remind you of dessert, but we eat it as a main course. Although Greeks usually don't like sweet main courses, Galatopita is very popular. Serve it as part of a buffet or as a dessert, if you prefer.

This is one dish that we usually make with homemade fyllo, though you can certainly use the commercial dough. One secret is to brush each sheet well with butter and then sprinkle it with sugar. When all the sheets are coated, press them down with your fingers. The result is a crisp, caramelized crust.

6 cups milk

6 large eggs

3 cups sugar

1 cup uncooked cream of wheat (semolina)

1½ tablespoons vanilla extract

5 tablespoons (⅓ stick) unsalted butter

1 tablespoon ground cinnamon

½ cup (1 stick) unsalted butter, melted and clarified (page 71)

½ pound fyllo dough

Preheat the oven to 400° F.

In a large saucepan, over medium heat, bring milk just to a boil. Meanwhile, in another large saucepan, beat eggs with 2½ cups of sugar until smooth. Add cream of wheat and mix well. Slowly pour in the hot milk, stirring constantly until well blended. Place the saucepan over medium heat and, still stirring, bring just to a boil; the consistency should be that of light cream. (Do not let the mixture boil vigorously or it will curdle.) Remove from heat and add vanilla, then butter, 1 tablespoon at a time, stirring until it melts.

Combine the remaining sugar and the cinnamon in a small bowl. With a pastry brush, coat a 9 by 13-inch baking pan with clarified butter. Place a sheet of fyllo dough in the bottom of the pan and brush it with clarified butter. Sprinkle with some of the cinnamon sugar. In this manner, layer all the fyllo sheets in the bottom of the pan, brushing each with butter and sprinkling with some of the cinnamon sugar. Press down on the layers with your fingers.

Pour the egg mixture on top of the fyllo. Bake for about 40 minutes, or until the custard is set and top is nicely browned. Serve hot or warm.

SERVES 8 TO 10

PEINIRLI *(Boat Pie)*

You might call this long boat of crusty dough a Greek calzone rather than a pita. *We rarely bake this at home, but we love to eat it at the tavernas. Just north of Athens, in Dionysos, are tavernas on both sides of the street with big signs advertising their special versions—a simple* peinirli *made with cheese or more elaborate ones filled with eggs, ham, bacon, mushrooms, sausages, onions, peppers, or ground meat. Peinirli is not really difficult to make; use this basic cheese recipe to create your own tasty specialties.*

4 cups all-purpose flour
Pinch of salt
1 ounce active dry yeast
½ cup warm water or more as
   needed

1 pound kasseri cheese, shredded
   (about 4 cups)
½ cup milk
6 tablespoons (¾ stick) unsalted
   butter

Put the flour and salt in a large bowl. Dissolve the yeast in warm water and add to the flour. Mix well, adding more warm water if necessary a tablespoon at a time to make a smooth and soft dough. Turn dough out onto a floured surface and knead for 5 minutes, until it is very soft, elastic, and velvety to the touch.

Place dough in a bowl, cover with a damp towel, and set aside in a warm area for 1½ hours, until the dough almost doubles in bulk. Uncover and punch down the dough. Divide the dough into 6 parts and shape into balls. Cover them with a damp towel and set aside in a warm area for another 30 minutes, until the dough again almost doubles in bulk.

Preheat the oven to 450° F.

Sprinkle a large baking sheet with flour. Shape the balls of dough into long loaves. Press firmly with your fingers to create an indentation down the centers of the loaves, so they resemble shallow boats. Arrange them on the baking sheet.

Mix the cheese with the milk. Fill the dough boats with the mixture and bake until the dough is crusty and golden, about 30 minutes. Place a tablespoon of butter on each boat and serve immediately.

SERVES 6

ELIOPITA *(Olive Pie)*

Actually more of an olive batter bread than a pie, this dish is popular in Cyprus. I first tasted it in a small taverna owned by Cypriots in downtown Athens, where it was served hot, with sliced ripe tomatoes and feta cheese on the side.

½ pound black Calamata olives, pitted and coarsely chopped
2 tablespoons finely chopped fresh mint, or 3 tablespoons dried

1 medium onion, finely chopped
3½ cups all-purpose flour
3 teaspoons baking powder
1 cup pure olive oil
2 cups warm water

Preheat the oven to 350° F.

Combine olives, mint, and onion in a bowl. In another bowl, combine the flour, baking powder, and olive oil. Slowly stir in warm water, mixing until the batter is smooth. Stir in the olive mixture.

Grease a 9 by 13-inch baking pan with a little olive oil and spread the batter in it. Bake for about 1 hour, or until evenly browned. Serve hot.

SERVES 6 TO 8

Desserts

(Glyka)

Anyone who has just consumed a filling Greek meal and thinks there's no room left for dessert may be mistaken. For instance, you may be surprised to learn that a Greek would almost never finish a meal with baklava, *either.*

Greeks have a somewhat different approach to desserts. For example, the term glyka *(dessert)* doesn't usually imply a finish to a meal. We call the last course the epithorpio, or epilogue, and on all but the most formal occasions it is fresh, seasonal fruit. In winter, my mother would sometimes serve baked apples or quinces sprinkled with sugar, brandy, and walnuts, but that's as close to a dessert as it got. Greeks prefer fruit at the end of a meal as a healthful, light balance to a good dinner; also, as we were growing up, this practice made us appreciate all the more the sweet desserts served on special occasions.

My mother, like all Greek housewives, always kept a store of cookies or biscota on hand to offer, along with coffee, to visitors during the day. Another treat always offered to visitors was homemade preserved fruit, which all Greek housewives dutifully put up in season. As for real desserts, Greeks have a tremendous variety prepared and served for different occasions and at different places.

You'll almost never find dessert on the menu at a small taverna. For cookies, cakes, pastries, marzipan, or ice cream, you would go to the zacharoplasteia (confectionary and pastry shop), and buy them to take out. If you wanted to sit and socialize over an iced coffee and a pastry such as a napoleon or cannoli, or a chocolate truffle, you'd seek out one of the many cafes.

Most of the recipes that follow, however, are for the glyka you would encounter when visiting someone's home on a special occasion, such as a party, birthday, wedding, Christmas, or Easter.

Frouta Psita me Karythia

(Baked Fruit)

On a cold winter night, this is a welcome variation of the fruit that we eat at the end of the meal. In this recipe, I use a combination of apples, quinces, and pears, but you can use just one type of fruit if you prefer.

2 large Golden Delicious apples
2 medium quinces
2 large pears
6 ounces walnuts, finely chopped
1 tablespoon ground cinnamon,
    plus ground cinnamon to taste
    for garnish

6 tablespoons sugar
1 cup brandy or cognac
2 tablespoons (¼ stick) unsalted
    butter
¾ cup water

Preheat the oven to 350° F.

Wash the fruit well. Core the fruit carefully, leaving the bottoms intact so that the stuffing will not fall out. Make the cavities large enough to hold several tablespoons of stuffing.

In a medium bowl, mix the walnuts, 1 tablespoon of cinnamon, and 3 tablespoons of sugar. Place the fruit upright in a small baking pan and stuff the centers with the mixture. Pour some brandy over each piece of fruit. Dot each piece with 1 teaspoon of butter and sprinkle each with 1½ teaspoons of sugar.

Pour water into the pan. Sprinkle the fruit with more cinnamon and bake for 45 to 60 minutes, or until all the fruit is soft when pierced with a fork and the sugar is caramelized on top. Serve warm.

SERVES 6

Kythoni Glyko tou Koutaliou

(Quince Spoon Dessert)

Greek spoon desserts are simply sweet preserves in syrup. There are countless variations of these preserves, from the more common fruit versions using quinces, orange or lemon peel, or sour cherries—to surprising concoctions of rose petals, baby eggplants, pistachios, or watermelon rind. A selection of spoon desserts is a must for any Greek household to keep on hand, for a small serving along with a cool glass of water is the traditional token of hospitality. I have found that some of these preserves also make wonderful toppings for ice cream or yogurt.

The recipe that follows calls for quinces, which are available only a few months in the fall. This is such a characteristic preserve, however, that it's worth waiting for the right season.

5 large ripe quinces
2½ cups water
6 cups sugar
1 tablespoon lemon juice

2 medium cinnamon sticks
4 scented geranium leaves, or 1
    vanilla bean (optional)

Wash the quinces. Cut into quarters, remove the cores, and cut into julienne strips or grate coarsely.

In a large pot, place the quinces, water, sugar, lemon juice, cinnamon, and geranium leaves or vanilla bean, if using. Simmer over medium heat, uncovered, stirring frequently, for at least 1½ hours, or until syrup is thick and quinces are slightly orange-pink and tender but not mushy. Let cool somewhat, then put into warmed pint jars. Cool completely before sealing the jars. Store the jars in the refrigerator.

MAKES ABOUT 2 PINTS

KOURABIETHES

(Almond Butter Cookies with Powdered Sugar)

The week before Christmas my mother would make big platters of these seasonal cookies, enough for all the friends and family who came to visit, enough to send to distant relatives, and even more to give to the neighborhood children who would come caroling.

1 cup (2 sticks) unsalted butter, at room temperature
¾ cup superfine sugar
2 egg yolks
2 tablespoons cognac or brandy
3 to 3½ cups all-purpose flour
2 teaspoons baking powder
½ cup shelled almonds, blanched, roasted, and coarsely chopped
1 pound confectioners' sugar

Preheat the oven to 300° F.

In a large bowl, beat the butter with an electric mixer, gradually adding the superfine sugar until the mixture is pale yellow and smooth. Beat in the egg yolks and brandy, then set aside.

In another bowl, sift together 3 cups of the flour and the baking powder. Beat this gradually into the butter mixture. Add the almonds and mix until dough is soft but not sticky. If dough still seems sticky, add up to ½ cup more flour.

Pinch off pieces of dough about the size of large walnuts and shape them into balls or crescents. Arrange them about 1 inch apart on a greased cookie sheet. Bake for about 20 minutes, until golden.

Sift half the confectioners' sugar onto a large platter. Place the hot cookies on top and sift the remaining sugar over them. Let cool for at least 2 hours. Serve or store in airtight tins for later use.

MAKES 30 TO 40 COOKIES

MELOMAKARONA

(Honey-Nut Cookies)

This is another cookie my mother used to make every Christmas. Even now, I think her Honey-Nut Cookies were the best I have ever had. Melomakarona *are a very old tradition. Some say the recipe came from the Phoenicians, which is why in some areas they are called* Phoenikia.

1 cup (2 sticks) unsalted butter, at
    room temperature
1½ cups pure olive oil
1½ cups sugar
1 cup orange juice
1 teaspoon grated orange peel

½ cup cognac or brandy
1 teaspoon ground cinnamon
⅓ teaspoon ground cloves
10 cups all-purpose flour
1 tablespoon baking powder
1 teaspoon baking soda

SYRUP
1 cup sugar
2 cups honey
2 cups water

1½ cups finely chopped walnuts
    for garnish

Preheat the oven to 300° F.

In the mixing bowl of an electric mixer, put the butter, oil, sugar, orange juice, orange peel, cognac, cinnamon, and cloves. Beat at medium speed for at least 30 minutes, until the mixture is smooth and creamy. This is easiest in a free-standing mixer.

In a large bowl, combine the flour, baking powder, and baking soda. Gradually beat flour into the butter mixture. The mixture will become too stiff for the mixer, at which point knead with your hands until the dough is well mixed and uniform. Turn it out onto a floured surface and knead the dough until it is smooth and soft.

Pinch off pieces of dough the size of a small egg and shape into ovals. Place ½ inch apart on a greased cookie sheet and use a fork to make an indented design. Bake for about 20 minutes, or until light brown. Let cool.

To make the syrup, put the sugar, honey, and water in a medium saucepan. Boil over medium heat for 5 to 8 minutes, or until the mixture becomes a thin syrup. Using a skimmer or slotted spoon, dip the cooled cookies into the hot syrup for about 1 minute. Roll immediately in chopped walnuts. Tightly sealed in aluminum foil, these cookies will keep for about 3 to 4 weeks.

MAKES APPROXIMATELY 70 COOKIES

KOULOURAKIA

(Special Occasion Cookies)

Koulourakia means any kind of cookie prepared for special occasions. This particular recipe is a favorite for Easter. Shape the dough into finger-size twists or crescents before baking.

2 cups all-purpose flour	¾ teaspoon baking powder
1 teaspoon ground cinnamon	½ teaspoon baking soda
¾ cup vegetable oil	¼ cup brandy
¾ cup superfine sugar	1 cup sesame seeds

Preheat the oven to 400° F.

Combine the flour and cinnamon in a bowl and set aside.

In a medium bowl, beat the oil and sugar with an electric mixer until smooth and creamy. In a cup, dissolve the baking powder and baking soda in the brandy, then add to the oil mixture.

Gradually add the flour until the dough is soft but not sticky. Turn out onto a lightly floured surface and knead until smooth. Pinch off pieces of dough the size of small walnuts and form into desired shapes. Sprinkle with sesame seeds and place 1 inch apart on greased cookie sheets. Bake for about 15 minutes, or until golden brown.

MAKES ABOUT 40 TO 50 COOKIES

AMYGTHALOTA *(Almond Cookies)*

Almonds are plentiful in Greece, especially throughout the islands, and this is one popular way to use them. These cookies are chewy, like meringues, but a lot denser because of the quantity of nuts.

6 egg whites
1½ cups confectioners' sugar
1 pound blanched almonds,
    finely chopped

Pinch of vanilla powder, or 1
    teaspoon vanilla extract

Preheat the oven to 350° F.

With an electric mixer, beat the egg whites until they are very stiff. Gradually add the sugar, almonds, and vanilla. Stir until the mixture is soft and uniform. With wet hands, pinch off pieces the size of walnuts and roll them into balls. Line a large baking sheet with wax paper and arrange the cookies on it 1 inch apart. Bake for about 15 minutes, until they rise and turn golden.

MAKES ABOUT 50 COOKIES

NOTE: These will keep for about 3 weeks, covered, in an airtight container.

BAKLAVA

This classic dessert, and the desserts on pages 158 and 160, are called glyka tapsiou, *or desserts baked in pans. They all call for fyllo dough and syrup, and there is one trick to making them: do not pour hot syrup on a hot dessert or the crust will get soggy. Always make sure that either the syrup or the dessert itself has cooled before you combine them.*

Although many people use only walnuts in making baklava, *I feel that a combination of almonds and walnuts lightens the dish. Old-fashioned* baklava *has a lot more sugar in it; this version will be a pleasant surprise to those who think of* baklava *as being almost too sweet to enjoy.*

8 ounces walnuts, finely ground
8 ounces almonds, finely ground
1 teaspoon ground cinnamon
¾ teaspoon ground cloves

1 tablespoon sugar
½ cup (1 stick) unsalted butter,
    melted and clarified (page 71)
1 pound fyllo pastry

SYRUP
3 cups sugar
2 thin lemon slices

4 cups water

Preheat the oven to 350° F.

In a medium bowl, thoroughly mix the walnuts, almonds, cinnamon, cloves, and sugar.

Grease a 9 by 13-inch baking pan with some of the clarified butter. Lay a sheet of fyllo dough in the bottom of the pan, brushing lightly with the butter. Layer 4 more sheets in the pan, brushing each lightly with butter. Sprinkle the fyllo with some of the nut mixture and cover with 2 more fyllo sheets, brushing each with butter. Sprinkle the fyllo with the nut mixture. Repeat the layers of fyllo and nuts until all the nut mixture is used, making 4 or 5 layers.

Cover the last layer of nuts with the 4 to 6 sheets of fyllo dough that should be left, again brushing each lightly with butter. Turn under the edges of the fyllo and score the surface into diamond-shaped serving pieces with a sharp knife. Bake for 45 to 60 minutes, or until golden brown. Remove from the oven and set aside to cool.

To make the syrup, put the sugar, lemon slices, and water in a large saucepan and boil over medium heat for 8 to 10 minutes. Remove lemon slices. The syrup should be thin but not watery. When the *Baklava* has cooled completely, pour the hot syrup over it. Let it stand for at least 3 hours before serving, so that the syrup is absorbed completely.

MAKES ABOUT 20 PIECES

EKMEK KADAIFI

(Kadaifi Custard Pie)

Introduced by Greeks from Asia Minor, this recipe was made with a kind of sweet bread instead of the kadaifi *dough. After baking the dessert, these Greeks would pour the syrup over it and then top it with* kaimaki, *a very thick whipped cream made from whole buffalo milk. Since I don't think you'll be able to find* kaimaki *here, or want to go to the trouble of making sweet bread for the crust, I have created this easier, lighter version.* Kadaifi *dough can be found ready-made in Midle Eastern markets or in some well-stocked grocery stores.*

1 pound *kadaifi* dough

½ cup (1 stick) unsalted butter, melted

SYRUP
2 cups granulated sugar
1 thin lemon slice
1 medium cinnamon stick
3 cups water

¼ pound almonds, blanched, roasted, and coarsely chopped

FILLING
4 cups milk
¾ cup cornstarch
1 cup granulated sugar
3 egg yolks, lightly beaten

3 tablespoons unsalted butter
½ teaspoon vanilla powder, or 1 tablespoon vanilla extract

MERINGUE
3 tablespoons confectioners' sugar
2 cups heavy cream

3 egg whites

Preheat the oven to 350° F.

Grease a round baking pan (12 to 14 inches in diameter) and spread the dough on the bottom. Pour the melted butter on top and bake for about 30 to 40 minutes, or until golden brown.

To make the syrup, put the granulated sugar, lemon slice, cinnamon stick, and water in a medium saucepan. Boil for 5 to 8 minutes, until the sugar dissolves but the syrup is still thin. Remove the lemon slice and cinnamon stick and slowly pour the syrup on top of the cooled pastry. Spread on this half the almonds and set aside.

To make the filling, heat 2 cups of the milk in a large saucepan. Put the remaining milk in a small bowl and dissolve the cornstarch and sugar in it. Add the mixture to the hot milk in the saucepan, constantly stirring with a wooden spoon over low heat until thick. Remove from the heat. Beat in the egg yolks, butter, and vanilla. The custard should be creamy and thick. If it is too thick, you may add a little cold milk.

To make the meringue, add the confectioners' sugar to the cream in a large bowl and beat with an electric mixer at high speed until stiff. In a medium bowl, beat the egg whites until stiff and fold them into the whipped cream.

Spread the custard over the pastry. Top with the meringue. Sprinkle with the remaining almonds. Serve at room temperature or chilled. The dessert will keep for several days, well covered, in the refrigerator.

MAKES 12 TO 15 PIECES

GALACTOBOUREKO *(Custard Fyllo Pie)*

You will notice that this recipe calls for cream of wheat, which simply is semolina, a common thickener in pies and desserts. Some people omit the semolina, but I find that it helps the dessert keep its shape when you slice it.

CUSTARD

4 cups milk
1 cup cream of wheat (semolina)
5 tablespoons sugar
5 egg yolks
½ teaspoon vanilla powder, or 1
    tablespoon vanilla extract

1 cup (2 sticks) unsalted butter,
    melted and clarified (page 71)
1 pound fyllo pastry

SYRUP

2 cups sugar
1 cinnamon stick

2 lemon slices
3 cups water

Preheat the oven to 350° F.

To make the custard, put the milk, cream of wheat, and sugar in a medium saucepan. Cook over low heat, stirring constantly until thick, about 10 to 15 minutes. Remove from the heat. Beat the egg yolks lightly and slowly fold them into the milk mixture. Add the vanilla and 2 tablespoons of the clarified butter and mix well.

With a pastry brush, grease a 9 by 13-inch baking pan with some of the clarified butter. Place a sheet of fyllo dough on the bottom of the pan and brush with the butter. Continue layering half the fyllo sheets in this manner, brushing each with butter. Pour in the custard filling and cover with the rest of the fyllo sheets, again brushing each sheet with some of the butter. Bake for about 30 minutes, or until golden brown.

In the meantime, make the syrup. Put sugar, cinnamon, lemon slices, and water in a medium saucepan and bring to a boil. Boil for 5 minutes, uncovered, until syrup begins thickening. Remove lemon slices and let syrup cool. When the hot *Galactoboureko* comes out of the oven, pour cooled syrup slowly over the top. Let cool completely before cutting and serving.

MAKES 12 TO 15 PIECES

TOURTA KASTANO *(Chestnut Pie)*

Chestnuts are popular in Greece. From November until the end of winter, they're sold hot from carts on almost every street corner, or you can buy them raw in the markets.

Around Christmas, my mother always made this special pie with brandy and chocolate. Although rich and high in calories, it makes a sensational dessert for a special dinner.

2 pounds chestnuts	⅔ cup cognac or brandy
2½ cups milk	6 ounces (about 30) ladyfingers
½ cup (1 stick) unsalted butter, softened	1½ cups heavy cream
1 cup superfine sugar	¾ cup confectioners' sugar
5 medium egg yolks	6 ounces semisweet chocolate, grated

Place chestnuts in a large saucepan. Cover generously with water and boil for about 40 minutes. Drain, and when the chestnuts are just cool enough to handle, peel them. Put the chestnuts and the milk in a large saucepan. Simmer over medium heat until the chestnuts are soft, about 30 minutes. Put chestnuts and milk in a food processor and puree until smooth.

In a large mixing bowl, cream the butter with an electric mixer, gradually adding the superfine sugar. Add the egg yolks and beat until the mixture is creamy and lemon-colored. Add the pureed chestnuts and mix well. Stir in 3 tablespoons of the cognac.

Cover the bottom of a 7- or 8-inch springform pan with ladyfingers and arrange more ladyfingers vertically around the sides. Sprinkle the remaining cognac over the ladyfingers and pour in the chestnut filling.

Combine the cream with the confectioners' sugar and beat with an electric mixer. Top pie with the whipped cream sprinkled with grated chocolate. Refrigerate for at least 1 hour before serving. Unmold the pie before serving.

SERVES 8 TO 10

KOLOKYTHOPITA GLYKA

(Sweet Pumpkin Pie)

From the end of fall until the beginning of spring, many kolokythes *(pumpkins) can be seen in Greek markets. Although different areas use them in a variety of dishes, in Thessalia we mostly use them in fyllo pies.*

One popular pumpkin pie is made with feta cheese and eggs, similar to the Zucchini Pie on page 136. My favorite version, however, is sweeter and flavored with cinnamon. Usually prepared for Lent, it is totally different from the pumpkin pie served for dessert in America.

When I was little, my job was to collect all the seeds from the pumpkins to make pasatempo *(pumpkin seed nibbles).* Pasatempo *means "pass the time," which is exactly what Greeks like to do with these salted pumpkin seeds, and with sunflower seeds as well.* Pasatempo *are sold on busy street corners, in dried fruit shops, and in movie theaters instead of popcorn. The snack is easy to make at home. Just wash the pumpkin seeds well and place them in a baking pan, sprinkle with water, and add about 1 teaspoon of salt for 3 cups of seeds. Put the seeds in a 200° F. oven to dry for about 2 hours. You can also dry them in the sun.*

1 medium pumpkin (about 4 pounds)	1½ cups bread crumbs
2 teaspoons salt	1 cup pure olive oil
1 cup dark raisins	1 cup sugar
1 cup finely chopped walnuts	Ground cinnamon to taste
	1 pound fyllo pastry

SYRUP

1½ cups water	2 lemon slices
2 cups sugar	

Cut open the pumpkin, discard the membranes and seeds (or make *pasatempo*), and cut the flesh into fist-size chunks. On the large holes of a hand grater, grate the flesh coarsely and discard the rind pieces. Sprinkle the grated pumpkin with salt and let it drain overnight in a colander.

The next morning, take a handful of the pumpkin at a time and squeeze out as much water as possible. Transfer the drained pumpkin to a large bowl and add the raisins, walnuts, bread crumbs, ¼ cup of the oil, sugar, and cinnamon. Mix well.

Preheat the oven to 350° F.

With a pastry brush, oil a 9 by 13-inch baking pan with some of the remaining oil. Lay a sheet of fyllo pastry in the pan and lightly brush it with oil. In this manner, layer 5 sheets of fyllo pastry in the bottom of the pan. Spread half the pumpkin mixture over the fyllo and cover with 5 more sheets of fyllo, lightly brushing each with oil. Spread the remaining pumpkin mixture on the fyllo and cover with 5 more sheets of fyllo, brushing each with oil. Brush the top generously with oil and score into serving squares with a sharp knife. Bake for about 1 hour, or until golden and crisp.

Meanwhile, make the syrup. Put the water, sugar, and lemon slices in a medium saucepan. Bring to a boil and cook for 5 to 10 minutes, or until syrup starts to thicken. Let the syrup cool.

Pour the cooled syrup over the hot pie. Serve warm.

SERVES 6 TO 8

VASILOPITA *(St. Basil's Pie)*

St. Basil's Day falls on New Year's Day, and the favorite festive dish in Greece is St. Basil's Pie. Traditionally a silver coin is hidden between the leaves of fyllo as the pie is being prepared. When the pie is served, everyone hopes to get the lucky piece with the coin. As a child I sometimes created such a fuss when I didn't get the coin that my mother had to hide another one in my piece.

The following recipe for St. Basil's Pie comes from Smyrna. (We in the region of Thessalia were exceptions to the custom of having a sweet pie for St. Basil's; our Vasilopita was always a cheese pie.) I had this version at a friend's New Year's Eve party in Thessaloniki and think it is very flavorful and light. Note that although we call this a pie, it looks more like an unfrosted cake. The top is usually decorated by snipping designs into the dough with scissors or using the tines of a fork. Then cloves are pressed in all over the surface of the cake.

1 cup (2 sticks) unsalted butter
1 cup sugar
4 large eggs, lightly beaten
¾ cup orange juice
½ cup cognac or brandy
2 teaspoons baking powder

1 teaspoon baking soda
5 cups all-purpose flour
1 egg, lightly beaten

Whole cloves (optional)

Preheat the oven to 350° F.

Beat the butter with the sugar in an electric mixer until creamy. Add the eggs and continue beating at medium speed for about 10 minutes.

In a medium bowl, combine juice, cognac, baking powder, and baking soda. Stir until well mixed. Pour into the butter mixture, beating all the while at medium speed until batter is smooth and light orange. Gradually add flour and knead dough with the mixer until soft and smooth. Turn out the dough, pat into a round shape, and place in a greased 12-inch round baking pan.

Brush the surface lightly with beaten egg. Press cloves all over the cake if desired. Bake for 50 to 60 minutes, until golden brown. Serve at room temperature.

SERVES 12 TO 15

POURA AMIGTHALOU *(Almond Cigars)*

Many of Greece's most delicious treats have come there through Macedonia and Asia Minor, and this is one more example. Poura Amigthalou *are individual, cigar-shaped fyllo pastries filled with a dense, almond mixture.*

1 pound blanched almonds,
    finely ground
2½ cups granulated sugar
¾ cup milk
½ teaspoon vanilla powder, or 1
    tablespoon vanilla extract
3 tablespoons Amaretto or other
    almond-flavored liquor

3 egg whites
½ cup (1 stick) unsalted butter
½ cup (1 stick) unsalted
    margarine
1 pound fyllo pastry
1 cup confectioners' sugar

Preheat the oven to 300° F.

In a large bowl, combine the almonds, sugar, milk, vanilla, and Amaretto. Using an electric mixer, beat the egg whites until stiff, then fold them into the almond mixture.

Melt and clarify the butter (see page 71) and melt the margarine, then combine and brush a sheet of fyllo with some of the mixture. Cut the fyllo sheet into quarters. Spread a tablespoon of the filling on each piece, turn in the edges, and firmly roll the pieces into thin "cigars." Repeat for the rest of the fyllo sheets. Place the cigars on a greased cookie sheet and brush the tops with a little more of the clarified butter-margarine mixture. Bake for about 30 minutes, or until golden brown. Remove from the oven and sprinkle with the confectioners' sugar.

MAKES APPROXIMATELY 60 "CIGARS"

MELAHRINI *(Brunette Cake)*

The combination of cognac and cinnamon in this dense, moist cake turns the batter a rich brown color—"brunette." In Thessalia, we always serve it at a wedding or other happy occasion.

8 large eggs, separated	1 cup fine white bread crumbs
2 cups sugar	½ teaspoon ground cinnamon
3 teaspoons baking powder	3 cups walnuts, finely ground
¼ cup cognac or brandy	

SYRUP

2 cups water	2 thin lemon slices
1½ cups sugar	

Preheat the oven to 300° F. Grease a 12-inch round baking pan.

In a large bowl, beat the egg yolks with an electric mixer. Gradually add the sugar and beat continuously until the mixture is thick and lemon-colored.

In a cup, dissolve the baking powder in the cognac. Add to the egg yolk mixture. Gradually add the bread crumbs, cinnamon, and walnuts. Beat the egg whites with an electric mixer until they are stiff and fold into the mixture. Pour the batter into the prepared pan and bake for about 40 to 50 minutes, or until the cake has risen and top is browned. Remove from oven and let cool in the pan.

To make the syrup, put the water, sugar, and lemon slices in a medium saucepan and bring mixture to a boil over medium heat. Boil for about 5 minutes, or until a thin but not watery syrup forms. Remove lemon slices. When the cake has cooled thoroughly, pour the hot syrup over it and cut into serving pieces.

SERVES 14 TO 16

KOPENHAGI *(Copenhagen Cake)*

Once, a long time ago, this cake might have come from Denmark, but Greeks added fyllo and syrup to the recipe and came up with a dessert that is certainly not served in Copenhagen. Nevertheless, the name remains.

5 large eggs, separated
¾ cup sugar
1 teaspoon grated lemon peel
¼ cup cognac or brandy
1 cup all-purpose flour
3 teaspoons baking powder
½ teaspoon ground cinnamon

1 pound blanched almonds,
    finely chopped
½ cup (1 stick) unsalted butter,
    melted and clarified (page 71)
¾ pound fyllo pastry

SYRUP
2½ cups water
2½ cups sugar

2 thin lemon slices

Preheat the oven to 350° F.

Using an electric mixer, beat the egg yolks with the sugar for about 10 minutes, until creamy and light yellow. Add the lemon peel and cognac.

Sift flour with baking powder and cinnamon. Add to the egg yolks and continue beating for at least 5 minutes, or until the mixture is smooth. Stir in the almonds. In a medium bowl, beat egg whites until stiff peaks form and fold into the batter.

Lay a sheet of fyllo dough in a greased, 9 by 13-inch baking pan and brush it lightly with some of the clarified butter. Repeat with 5 more sheets of fyllo, lightly buttering each. Pour the batter onto the fyllo pastry and cover with 5 more sheets of fyllo, again brushing each lightly with clarified butter. With a sharp knife, score the fyllo dough into diamond-shaped serving pieces. Bake for about 45 to 60 minutes, until golden brown. Let cool.

To make the syrup, put water, sugar, and lemon slices in a medium saucepan. Bring to a boil over medium heat and boil for about 5 minutes, or until a thin, but not watery, syrup forms. Remove the lemon slices. Pour the hot syrup over the cool pastry and let stand for at least 1 hour before serving.

SERVES 14 TO 16

REVANI *(Semolina Delight)*

The Macedonians make this moist, dense cake the best, as they do many other sweets. Adapted from a Turkish recipe, Revani *is so popular in northern Greece that it used to be sold by the slice outside movie theaters and concert halls.*

6 large eggs, separated

2 cups sugar

3 cups cream of wheat (semolina)

2 teaspoons baking powder

½ teaspoon baking soda

2 cups plain yogurt

1 cup blanched almonds, coarsely chopped

SYRUP

4 cups water

2½ cups sugar

2 thin lemon slices

Preheat the oven to 350° F. Butter a 9-inch round or square baking dish.

In a large bowl, beat the egg yolks and sugar with an electric mixer until they are creamy and smooth, about 5 minutes.

In another bowl, mix the cream of wheat with the baking powder and soda. Alternately, add the yogurt and the cream of wheat mixture to egg yolks, beating well after each addition, until ingredients are well blended.

With an electric mixer, beat the egg whites until they are stiff. Fold them into the batter, which should look foamy and light. Pour the batter into the prepared baking pan, sprinkle with almonds, and bake for about 45 minutes. Let cool.

To make the syrup, put the water, sugar, and lemon slices in a large saucepan and bring to a boil over medium heat. Continue boiling for 5 to 8 minutes, or until a thin, but not watery, syrup forms. Remove the lemon slices. When the cake has cooled, pour the hot syrup over it and let it stand for at least 1 hour before serving.

SERVES 8

YIAOURTOPITA *(Yogurt Cake)*

Think of this as a pound cake, with the Greek twist of yogurt. Topped with its white frosting, Yiaourtopita *is delicious served with coffee.*

1 cup (2 sticks) unsalted butter, softened to room temperature
1½ cups sugar
4 large eggs, separated
½ teaspoon vanilla powder, or 1 tablespoon vanilla extract

4 cups all-purpose flour
1 tablespoon plus 1 teaspoon baking powder
1½ cups plain yogurt
Pinch of salt

FROSTING
½ cup warm water
1 cup sugar
⅓ teaspoon cream of tartar

2 egg whites
½ teaspoon vanilla powder, or 1 tablespoon vanilla extract

Preheat the oven to 350° F. Butter a 9 by 13-inch baking pan and set aside.

Using an electric mixer, cream the butter while gradually adding the sugar, egg yolks, and vanilla.

In a large bowl, sift the flour with the baking powder. Alternately add the flour and yogurt to the butter mixture, beating well after each addition.

With an electric mixer and clean beaters, beat the egg whites with the salt until they form stiff peaks. Fold the whites into the batter. Pour the batter into the prepared pan and bake for about 40 minutes, or until risen and golden brown. Remove cake from the oven and let cool. Transfer to a serving platter.

To make the frosting, put the water, sugar, and cream of tartar in a saucepan and bring to a boil over medium heat. Continue boiling for about 3 minutes, or until the syrup starts to thicken. Remove from heat. With an electric mixer, beat the egg whites until they form stiff peaks. While the syrup is still hot, pour it slowly into the whites, stirring well. The mixture should be thick and glossy. Add the vanilla and mix well. Top the cake with the frosting and serve.

SERVES 8 TO 10

BOUGATSA

Another dish brought to Greece by immigrants from Asia Minor, Bougatsa *is very similar to the Thessalian* Galatopita *(Milk Pie, page 143), except that* bougatsa *is eaten as a dessert. Especially in Thessaloniki, there are many tiny shops called* bougetsadzithika *that display huge* bougatsas *in copper pans. Each order is freshly cut in front of you, placed on a piece of wax paper, and sprinkled lavishly with confectioners' sugar and cinnamon. At home, though, I prefer to make this* Bougatsa *in small, individual servings.*

2 cups milk

3 tablespoons all-purpose flour

4 tablespoons plus 2 teaspoons granulated sugar

2 teaspoons cornstarch

2 medium egg yolks

4 tablespoons (½ stick) unsalted butter

½ teaspoon vanilla powder, or 1 tablespoon vanilla extract

2 tablespoons blanched and slivered almonds

3 large Golden Delicious apples, peeled, cored, and diced

½ teaspoon ground cinnamon

6 5-inch squares of *sfoliata* (puff pastry)

Confectioners' sugar and ground cinnamon for garnish

Heat 1½ cups of milk in a medium saucepan. Meanwhile, combine the flour, 3 tablespoons granulated sugar, and cornstarch in a bowl. Whisk in the remaining ½ cup milk and the egg yolks. Whisk the mixture into the heated milk and bring to a boil over medium heat, stirring with a wooden spoon until it is thick and creamy. Remove from the heat. Beat in 1½ tablespoons of the butter and the vanilla. Fold in the almonds.

In a heavy skillet, melt the remaining butter over medium heat. Add the apples and cook until soft, stirring frequently, about 5 to 10 minutes. Sprinkle with remaining granulated sugar and continue cooking until lightly caramelized and golden. Sprinkle with cinnamon. Stir the apples into the custard and set aside to cool.

Preheat the oven to 350° F. Roll out each piece of pastry on a lightly floured surface into 7-inch squares. Spoon equal amounts of filling in the center of each square, then fold pastry in half to form 7 by 3½-inch rectangles and pinch edges to seal.

Place on a greased baking sheet and bake until golden brown and puffy, about 30 minutes. Remove from the oven and sprinkle with confectioners' sugar and cinnamon. Serve immediately.

SERVES 6

RIZOGALO *(Rice Pudding)*

Because it is such a simple dish, I am constantly surprised by the number of Americans who appreciate and ask for Greek rice pudding. Perhaps its simplicity is the key: Greek rice pudding is very light, with no butter or eggs. We often eat it as a light snack in the early evening or have it with coffee at the neighborhood kaffeneia.

6 tablespoons long-grain white rice	1 cup sugar
1½ cups water	Small piece of lemon peel
6 cups milk	½ teaspoon vanilla powder, or 1
3 tablespoons cornstarch	tablespoon vanilla extract
4 tablespoons warm water	Ground cinnamon to taste

Wash the rice well and drain. Put it in a large saucepan with the water and bring to a boil. Cover and simmer over medium-low heat until most of the water evaporates, about 10 minutes. Add the milk and simmer for about 15 minutes more.

In a cup, dissolve the cornstarch in warm water. Add this to the rice mixture along with the sugar and lemon peel. Stir constantly over medium-low heat until the mixture turns into a thick and creamy pudding, about 10 to 15 minutes. Remove the lemon peel and stir in the vanilla.

Pour into individual bowls, sprinkle with cinnamon, and serve warm or chilled.

SERVES 6 TO 8

MARENGES *(Meringues with Metaxa Brandy)*

This lovely summer dessert is reminiscent of an English trifle. The fruit is flavored with Metaxa, the classic Greek brandy, available in most liquor stores.

2 cups fresh raspberries, or your
  choice of berries
½ cup Metaxa brandy
¼ cup granulated sugar

2 cups heavy cream
½ cup confectioners' sugar
½ teaspoon vanilla powder, or 1
  tablespoon vanilla extract

MERINGUES
2 egg whites, at room temperature
  Pinch of salt
⅔ cup superfine sugar
1 teaspoon distilled white vinegar

⅓ teaspoon vanilla powder, or ¾
  tablespoon vanilla extract

1 cup coarsely chopped roasted
  almonds for garnish

In a medium bowl, combine the raspberries, brandy, and sugar. Set aside. In another bowl, combine the heavy cream with confectioners' sugar and vanilla, and beat with an electric mixer until it forms soft peaks. Refrigerate.

Preheat the oven to 200° F. Line a baking sheet with foil and grease the foil with butter.

To make the meringues, beat the egg whites and salt with an electric mixer until soft peaks form. Gradually add the sugar and beat until whites are stiff and glossy. Carefully fold in the vinegar and vanilla.

Spoon generous tablespoons of the meringue mixture onto the prepared baking sheet. Lightly flatten the tops with the back of the spoon. Bake for about 1 hour, or until lightly colored and dry. Turn off the oven and let the meringues cool in the unopened oven for at least 3 hours to completely dry.

In a large glass serving bowl, layer half the raspberry mixture (undrained), half the whipped cream, and half the meringues. Spread the remaining raspberries over this, then the whipped cream, and finish with the meringues. Sprinkle the chopped almonds on top and serve immediately. Do not let the dessert sit too long, or the meringues will become soggy.

SERVES 6 TO 8

THIPLES *(Fritters)*

These honey-dipped fritters, flavored with brandy and orange juice, are another part of our Christmas tradition.

5 large eggs
2 tablespoons (¼ stick) unsalted butter
⅓ cup milk
2 tablespoons cognac or brandy
2 tablespoons orange juice

1 tablespoon baking powder
2½ cups all-purpose flour
½ teaspoon salt
3 cups vegetable oil for deep-frying

SYRUP
1 cup sugar
1 cup honey
2 cups water

1 cup finely chopped walnuts, and ground cinnamon for garnish

Beat the eggs well with an electric mixer. Gradually add the butter, milk, cognac, orange juice, baking powder, flour, and salt and beat until the dough is soft and smooth. Divide the dough into 4 parts and roll each out into a square about ⅛ inch thick. With a pastry wheel or pizza cutter, cut each square into 2-inch square pieces.

In a deep skillet or fryer, heat the oil until very hot but not smoking. Fry the dough pieces until they turn light golden, about 2 minutes. Remove with a skimmer or slotted spoon and drain on paper towels.

To make the syrup, put the sugar, honey, and water in a medium saucepan and boil for 5 to 8 minutes. The syrup should still be thin, but not watery. Carefully drop the *Thiples* in the hot syrup, remove with a skimmer, and place on a serving platter. Sprinkle with walnuts and cinnamon and serve.

MAKES ABOUT 50 FRITTERS

TSOUREKIA *(Easter Sweet Bread)*

This is the crowning glory of the big Easter meal, but it is also a treat to have the leftovers the following week. The sweet, flavorful bread is delicious thinly sliced for breakfast or as a snack with coffee. To be authentic, you'll need to find an aromatic seed called mahlepi, *which the Greeks adapted from the Turks and always use in their* Tsourekia. *It's usually available in Middle Eastern markets, but if you can't find it, don't worry. The bread will still be delicious.*

1 cup milk
2 tablespoons active dry yeast
9 cups all-purpose flour
1 tablespoon *mahlepi*, dissolved in
    ⅓ cup lukewarm water
    (optional)
1 teaspoon salt
1 cup (2 sticks) unsalted butter,
    melted

8 large eggs, at room temperature
2 cups sugar
1 tablespoon grated orange rind

Halved blanched almonds and
    sesame seeds for garnish

In a small saucepan, warm the milk, add the yeast, and stir to dissolve. Add about 3 tablespoons of the flour and stir until a thick paste forms. Cover with a tea towel and put in a warm place. Let rise until double in bulk, about 30 minutes.

Put the remaining flour in a large bowl along with the *mahlepi*, if using. Add the salt, butter, 6 of the eggs, sugar, orange rind, and yeast mixture. Knead until the dough is soft, smooth, and elastic. Cover the bowl with a tea towel and let stand in a warm place until the dough has doubled in bulk, about 2 hours. Uncover and knead again for a couple of minutes.

Punch dough and divide into eighths. The traditional shape for *Tsourekia* is a braided loaf, but you can form the loaves in any shape you wish. Place the loaves on greased baking sheets, keeping in mind that they will double in size. Cover with a tea towel and put in a warm place until doubled in bulk again, about 1 hour.

Preheat the oven to 400° F.

Beat the remaining 2 eggs lightly and brush them over the risen bread loaves. Sprinkle with almonds and sesame seeds. Bake for about 30 minutes. Let cool before slicing.

MAKES 8 LOAVES

NOTE: This bread keeps wonderfully in the freezer for up to 2 months when tightly wrapped in plastic.

LOUKOUMATHES *(Honey Balls)*

Shaped either like small balls or little rings, these fritters, dipped in hot honey syrup, are like Greek doughnuts. My mother made them at home, especially around Christmas, but they are also readily available year-round from the loukoumatzithika, *or shops that specialize in them.*

½ ounce active dry yeast	5 cups vegetable oil, for deep-frying
3 cups lukewarm water	
3 cups all-purpose flour	About 1 cup honey, and ground
Pinch of salt	cinnamon for garnish

Dissolve the yeast in ½ cup warm water. Put the flour in a large bowl and stir in the yeast. Gradually add more lukewarm water (about 2½ cups) until mixture has the consistency of a smooth, thick cake batter. Add salt and stir well.

Cover the batter with a wet towel and let it stand in a warm place for about 1 hour, or until it has almost doubled in bulk.

In a deep skillet or fryer, heat the oil until it is very hot but not smoking. Drop teaspoonfuls of the batter into the hot oil and fry until golden brown, about 2 minutes. After each spoonful, dip the teaspoon in cold water to keep the batter from sticking.

Remove the *Loukoumathes* from oil as they are done and place on paper towels to drain. Place on a serving dish, drizzle with honey and dust with cinnamon, then serve hot.

MAKES 25 TO 30 HONEY BALLS

INDEX

CONVERSION CHART

Equivalent Imperial and Metric Measurements

American cooks use standard containers, the 8-ounce cup and a tablespoon that takes exactly 16 level fillings to fill that cup level. Measuring by cup makes it very difficult to give weight equivalents, as a cup of densely packed butter will weigh considerably more than a cup of flour. The easiest way therefore to deal with cup measurements in recipes is to take the amount by volume rather than by weight. Thus, the equation reads:

1 cup = 240 ml = 8 fl. oz.   ½ cup = 120 ml = 4 fl. oz.

It is possible to buy a set of American cup measures in major stores around the world.

In the States, butter is often measured in sticks. One stick is the equivalent of 8 tablespoons. One tablespoon of butter is therefore the equivalent to ½ ounce/15 grams.

Linear Measure

1 inch	2.54 centimeters
1 foot	0.3048 meters
1 yard	0.9144 meters

Area Measure

1 square inch	6.4516 square centimeters
1 square foot	929.03 square centimeters
1 square yard	0.836 square meters

Liquid Measures

FLUID OZ.	U.S.	IMPERIAL	MIL.
	1 TSP	1 TSP	5
¼	2 TSP	1 DESSERTSPOON	7
½	1 TBS	1 TBS	15
1	2 TBS	2 TBS	28
2	¼ CUP	4 TBS	56
4	½ CUP OR ¼ PINT		110
5		¼ PINT OR 1 GILL	140
6	¾ CUP		170
8	1 CUP OR ½ PINT		225
9			250, ¼ LITER
10	1¼ CUPS	½ PINT	280
12	1½ CUPS OR ¾ PINT		340
15		¾ PINT	420
16	2 CUPS OR 1 PINT		450
18	2¼ CUPS		500, ½ LITER
20	2½ CUPS	1 PINT	560
24	3 CUPS OR 1½ PINTS		675
25		1¼ PINTS	700
27	3½ CUPS		750
30	3¾ CUPS	1½ PINTS	840
32	4 CUPS OR 2 PINTS OR 1 QUART		900
35		1¾ PINTS	980
36	4½ CUPS		1000, 1 LITER
40	5 CUPS OR 2½ PINTS	2 PINTS OR 1 QUART	1120
48	6 CUPS OR 3 PINTS		1350
50		2½ PINTS	1400
60	7½ CUPS	3 PINTS	1680

Solid Measures

U.S. AND IMPERIAL		METRIC	
OUNCES	POUNDS	GRAMS	KILOS
1		28	
2		56	
3½		100	
4	¼	112	
5		140	
6		168	
8	½	225	
9		250	¼
12	¾	340	
16	1	450	
18		500	½
20	1¼	560	
24	1½	675	
27		750	¾
28	1¾	780	
32	2	900	
36	2¼	1000	1
40	2½	1100	
48	3	1350	
54		1500	1½
64	4	1800	
72	4½	2000	2
80	5	2250	2¼
90		2500	2½
100	6	2800	2¾

Suggested Equivalents and Substitutes for Ingredients

all-purpose flour—plain flour
arugula—rocket
beet—beetroot
confectioner's sugar—icing sugar
cornstarch—cornflour
eggplant—aubergine
granulated sugar—caster sugar
lima beans—broad beans
scallion—spring onion
shortening—white fat
squab—poussin
squash—courgettes or marrow
unbleached flour—strong, white flour
vanilla bean—vanilla pod
zest—rind
zucchini—courgettes
light cream—single cream
heavy cream—double cream
half and half—12% fat milk
cheesecloth—muslin

Oven Temperature Equivalents

FAHRENHEIT	CELSIUS	GAS MARK	DESCRIPTION
225	110	¼	
250	130	½	Cool
275	140	1	Very Slow
300	150	2	
325	170	3	Slow
350	180	4	Moderate
375	190	5	
400	200	6	Moderately Hot
425	220	7	Fairly Hot
450	230	8	Hot
475	240	9	Very Hot
500	250	10	Extremely Hot

Any broiling recipes can be used with the grill of the oven, but beware of high-temperature grills.